The Book of Love

Published by Expressive Egg Books

Copyright © 2025 Darren Allen. All rights reserved. Subject to statutory exception and to the provisions of relevant collective licensing agreements, no part of this book may be reproduced in any manner without the prior written permission of the author and publisher.

Darren Allen has asserted his moral rights under the Copyright, Designs and Patents Act 1988.

Cover design, Darren Allen

Set in Skolar 10pt on a 12pt line
with 14pt Futura headings

ISBN: 978-1-7391294-6-0 (paperback)
978-1-7391294-7-7 (epub)

Disclaimer: the author accepts
no liability for actions inspired by this book
unless they are extremely funny.

10 9 8 7 6 5 4 3 2 1

Yes, love is a real magician. One has only to
love, and what one loves becomes beautiful.

> Leo Tolstoy

Where I touch you, I flame into being;
but is it me, or you?

> D.H. Lawrence

How blest am I in this discovering thee!
To enter in these bonds, is to be free.

> John Donne

The woman penetrated is a labyrinth. Man
emerges into another world inside her.

> Norman O. Brown

Men die to get away from women;
and are reborn to join them.

> Barry Long

I cry, Love! Love! Love! happy happy Love! free
as the mountain wind!

> William Blake

Contents

Introduction	9
A Note on the Text	11
Sex and Gender	13
Man and Woman	15
Speaking of Love	29
The World's War on Love	31
Attachment and Resistance	35
Sex and Getting Off	40
Two Kinds of Perversion	42
The World is Fucked	45
Primal and Civilised Love	48
Emotion and Feeling	51
Ideology and Habit	55
Improvisation and Fate	58
Conversation and Courtship	63
The Fiendess	69
Sex with your Self	72
Male and Female Sexuality	78

Life, Play and Passion	80
Courage and Sensitivity	85
Man on the Moon	88
Making Love	93
Submission and Domination	99
After the Honeymoon	102
The Bond of Fear	104
Caricatures and Cyphers	106
Fitting and Suiting	110
A Ritual of Commitment	114
A Brief History of Marriage	116
Postmodern Couplings	120
Eternal Love	123
Acceptance and Action	125
The Flesh of Eternity	127
Vigilance and Courage	130
The End and the Beginning	134
Endnotes	139

Introduction

The number of intelligent books on the subject of gender, sex, love, courtship and marriage approaches zero. Readers hoping to understand what love is, or what it means to be a man or a woman, or why sex is so often painful and disappointing, or how to approach or be approached by a member of the opposite sex, or why modern attitudes to sex and gender are so fraught with contention, will search bookshops in vain. This is partly because the cultural elite, the professional class who control what appears in bookshops (and on television and in newspapers), do not understand sex, love, and gender, and are threatened by any serious or perceptive attempt to do so. But, as we shall see, their ostensible opponents on the right are just as ignorant of love, they just express their fears in a different way. In the end, everyone gets anxious and defensive when the subject comes up.

Love in this respect (and, as has often been noted, in many other respects) is much like death. We joke about death, we sentimentalise it, but nobody seriously talks about it, for the simple reason that we are ashamed that there is no place for death in our lives. And just as nobody sees dead bodies, handles them, or ever really faces the physical fact of death, so nobody feels love, knows anyone who is in love, or ever really addresses the reality of love as it actually is. We intuitively know that this is shameful, and so when love, sex or gender come up in conversation, or if we pick up a book that challenges our carefully managed opinions, we get emotional, we feel anxious, and then either fall into silly arguments, or euphemistically skirt around the subject.

The book you are reading does not skirt around the subject of love. It faces it head-on. Not as an object of scientific inquiry, not as a subjective stroll through my love life and not as a justification for my ideological position, but simply and directly. What I have to say about love is consonant with the facts of science (for example, the observed differences in the male and female brain), it emerges from my personal experience and it takes what truth there is in both left- and right-wing attitudes to sex and gender. But the truth of love is neither socialist nor capitalist, neither objective nor subjective. It flies above science and it digs beneath art. It rejects both the modern left-wing image of love as a polite union of two fundamentally identical, or equal, civilians *and* the pre-modern right-wing image of love as a perennial battle between two very different beasts.

This book is therefore offensive to everyone with an ideological position. You can't hold a position in love. Love is too strange, too real, to be pinned down by an ideology or a mere opinion, no matter how well established in fact. Imagine saying to someone, 'I *believe* I love you' or 'my *opinion* is that I love you,' or 'I can *prove* I love you.' Such utterances strike us as appalling because we all know, somewhere deep inside, that love is elusive, rich with quality, and, ultimately, mysterious. We know this, but when love speaks, we reach for beliefs, opinions and facts.

This is why I say that this is a 'radical' guide to love, sex, and gender. It does not provide you with something to believe in, or a decidedly unmysterious attitude, nor even does it *add* much to you in the way of literal knowledge. What this book aims to do is get at the root[1] of our confusion, which means to *take away* what stands between you and your extraordinary nature. This may well be an unsettling experience. It might trigger your fears and addictions and make you get emotional, but if you listen, it will take you somewhere new. Just as love does.

A Note on the Text

The Book of Love book has been written to be readable and easy to digest, which means that a few bald statements have been left to stand on their own. I have put supporting arguments, references, quotes and a few digressions into the endnotes, which are a little fuller and more interesting than you might expect.

Sex and Gender

The words MAN and WOMAN refer to sexual *facts*. Men actively produce sperm (up to two trillion) and women are passively born with eggs (about four or five hundred). These primal facts have qualities, as all facts do, which is why men are always basically (or qualitatively) masculine, and women are always basically feminine.

The words MASCULINE and FEMININE, however, refer not to sexual facts, but to gendered *qualities* which, as all primal people (and great artists) well understood, can inhere in any kind of fact, even in numbers. This is why, for example, cats feel more feminine than dogs, which feel more masculine.[1]

Upon the *primal facts* of man or woman, the self comprises an infinite number of *secondary facts*, with their own polar, gendered qualities. I call these 'secondary facts' MODALITIES. These pertain to mind, will, body and feeling, each of which can be 'shaded' with more or less masculinity or femininity.

Woman then is ultimately feminine, and man is ultimately masculine, but each is made up of many, various and extremely subtle gendered modalities. A man can have a slightly feminine jaw, for example, or a feminine attitude to authority, while a woman can have a touch of masculinity in her sexuality, and so on.

Thus a *balanced* human is *primarily* either male or female, with, following from this, a massive and highly nuanced variety of *secondary* modalities. Together, all these qualities make up the fascinating blend, in all human beings, between the essential or general man and woman, and the specific, unique individual.

Secondary modalities can be culturally acquired; they are shaped by environments which can also be masculine or feminine.[2] Thus, *balanced* (or *primal*) societies produce essentially masculine men and essentially feminine women, with, again, an immense variety of subtle and interesting modalities following from this.

Unbalanced societies either produce overly masculine men and feminine women (such PSEUDO-GENDERED people tend to appear in pre-modern, moralistic societies) or they produce overly feminine men and overly masculine women (such MONO-GENDERED people tend to appear in postmodern, decadent societies).

Opposites attract, which is why a partner is most attractive when they have complementary modalities. A projective masculine mind will enjoy the company of a receptive feminine mind, a sharp, square masculine body will find a soft, round feminine form attractive, and so on and so forth.

Although it is considered a thoughtcrime today, it is possible to make general observations[3] about men, those people who produce sperm, and about women, those people who are born with eggs, and about the masculine and the feminine, qualities which most—but not all—men and women essentially possess.

But generalisations are gestures. To speak of the essential difference between man and woman one must, as Ivan Illich pointed out, reach for metaphor, because sex and gender refer to *complementary qualities* that are, rationally speaking, enigmatic. It is impossible to 'pin down' man and woman.

There is no true, enigmatic, love without this complementarity. If you are basically the same as me, I may like you, understand you; but I cannot experience a mystery that unites, as metaphors do, two different qualities. Love becomes mathematical, or rationally understandable. Unmysterious. Economic.

Man and Woman

Have you ever noticed how, when a man and woman in relationship argue, if he is found to be wrong, he often seems to be *more* wrong than she does when she's guilty? Have you ever sensed a tragic quality of corrupted innocence about even the most horrendous women, something that male monsters do not have?

It's simple. It's his fault. Ultimately, it's all his fault. Adam fell first, and then he blamed Eve, and he has been blaming her ever since. Woman is responsible, of course — in fact, she takes on the evil in the world more readily than man does, and becomes far more deranged — but the source of it all, is in his stinking heart.

Every man has a devil in him. An angel too, yes, but the fiend that man nurses in his self (even — sometimes especially — the nicest and most likeable men) makes the evil of woman appear, if not more trivial (for she can certainly be grotesquely wicked), then, at the very least, more pitiful.[1]

Woman, generally speaking, is more innocent than man. She is more gullible than man, more childlike, more trusting, more spontaneous, more sensitive and more compassionate. This is because she is born *whole*. Man, as primal people recognise, is born incomplete, with an insensitive split, and must learn to become whole, in time.

The fundamental unity of the child's self with the mother's body means that, as man grows he becomes conscious of a fundamental *difference* and must discover what he is by looking outwards, into society. The maturing woman, by contrast, knows that, fundamentally, she is what she already is. She has no need to 'go' anywhere.

This explains many of the basic psychological differences between man and woman. He presses forward, she holds back, he focuses on the part and she takes in the whole. It also explains, as we shall see, how man is deranged by abandoning his search for his self in the world and she is deranged *by* being forced to *be* someone.[2]

Man thus has ASPIRATION, something which is basically alien to woman. She may aspire, but she doesn't have the need to find or master herself in worldly activity. This is why feminine women tend to give up on the path to mastery. They become good, but they almost never become great. Anyone who says otherwise has no taste.[3]

A woman with personal aspiration is either unhappy or angry. Woman does not need to aspire to completeness.[4] What she needs to do is refuse to compromise with a loveless — which is to say, incomplete—life. This is the only real rift in her existence, and the only thing, aside from the love of man, she naturally 'aspires' to.[5]

This is unsayable in the unnatural world. The possibility that there is something that women might desire beyond worldly career or technical mastery must be taken as bigotry by a world which demands woman's competitive participation, and which also demands she deform herself to competitively participate.

Men are not really interested in women who strive. Okay, so she has an ambition, fine. Lovely. Women, however, hate men who do not strive. He doesn't have to aspire to some marvellous cultural achievement, but if there is no sense in him that he is seeking to overcome his self, she'll unconsciously hate him.

All this explains why it is so important for woman to *respect* man—for what he has achieved, for how he lives, for what he values—but so unimportant for man to do likewise. Woman asking for respect is asking for trouble, because she wants something that man will not give her until she is in her seventies.

Another aspect of aspiration is *individuality*. The aspiration of man to overcome his self pulls him out of the crowd, although man is naturally more individual than woman anyway—and seeks individuality more than she does—which is why women's faces naturally resemble each other more than men's do.[6]

Overcoming self means discovering some 'part' of your conscious experience that transcends will, mind, body and emotion (a 'part' women have no need to find, because she *is* that[7]). Man does this through love (for nature, for woman, for the ineffable) and through mastering his tools in worldly activity.

In mastering his tools—including the tool of his mind—man learns to master himself. Industrial technology and institutions are not TOOLS, they are SYSTEMS, and cannot be mastered (they master us), which is why guitarists are more desirable than managers and why women do not fawn over professional gamers.

Men who do not master themselves seek to master other selves. This explains the striking similarity between the attitude of unconscious men towards both nature and women, as external things to be studied, experimented on and used, for one's own benefit, rather than as mysteries to be experienced, from within.

Such men are rightly considered to be, by women, simple creatures.[8] This is because they do not have a very noble aspiration or are not far enough advanced in their pursuit of self-discovery. They are children, and she treats them as such. A man who knows what he is about is almost as subtle and strange as a woman. Almost!

All real women have PhDs in aspiration discernment. They can tell from sniffing the air if a man's aspiration is coming from his innermost, if he really knows what he wants, or if he's struggling to acquire an external talent, power or USP. She's not concerned with his stats, but with his basic nobility or integrity.

Man must aspire to his own fate, to the discovery of what the Hindus and Buddhists call *dharma*, which is not mere duty, and certainly not selfish desire, but a difficult and painful process (a HERO'S JOURNEY) of self-discovery, and a courageous endeavour to realise the fruits of self-discovery in the selfish, and purposeless, world.

None of which is really necessary for woman. Today, we live in a world in which women are forced to aspire, to succeed and, most unnaturally of all (for her), to *win*. She really doesn't give a damn about winning, but she has to in the man-made world. All this disturbs her spirit, particularly when she is menstruating.

Woman is also forced to hyper-focus in the world—another male trait. She *must* pick out things in the world and manipulate them. Obviously she can do this, and even enjoy doing it, but the degree to which she is *compelled* to abstract in this way corrupts her embodied presence and wisdom, and makes her male.

Acquisitive and competitive women are, increasingly, in control of the world, but woman cannot change the male-made essence of the world. It changes her. It infects her with an unnatural, projective, abstract, insensitive and disembodied maleness, which she then defends as her nature and her right.

The most conspicuous *physical* manifestation of woman's acquired maleness is her tragic lack of SENSUALITY. Modern woman, in man's world, has less and less sensuous presence, which makes her more and more emotional; more depressed, more anxious, more frustrated, more angry,[9] and less feminine.

(And what knight wants to rescue another man from the dragon? What man is prepared to go through hell for a *policewoman*?[10] This isn't to say it's her fault that man has lost his spirit, courage and chivalry, that he no longer wishes to rise to the noble challenge of being worthy of her, but neither is she guiltless.)

The most conspicuous *social* manifestation of woman's acquired maleness is FEMINISM. Feminism can mean a simple desire to help women, but the word as it is officially (and commonly) used refers to an ideological technique for forcing woman into man's working world, where he can more easily manipulate her. Feminism serves man.

Although it is true that once, in the 'bad old days' of the pre-modern past, men wielded ruthless power over women's lives, it is also true that women once had power over her DOMAIN, the home, which she has now lost. Now, with the exception of a few privileged women in the West, she is powerless everywhere.

If you ask young women in the West today, 'Do we need men?' many will cry, 'No!' Not because she can do everything he can do (such as all the gruelling physical professions dominated by men[11]), but because his technological system has made him (and her) obsolete. When it falls apart, as it soon will, her answer will quickly change.

Now man might be under her thumb at home *and* in the office, but this is a Pyrrhic victory if ever there was one. Not only has her power over him eroded the love between them, but the man-made system now rules over her completely, over her mind and body, everywhere, and she helped that happen.

Woman might be more innocent and loving than men, but she is as responsible as he is for the loveless state of the world, because she compromises so readily with it. She accepts lovelessness; through fear of being abandoned, through lack of confidence in love and through her perverse addiction to emotion.

Man plays on this emotion. First of all he undermines her confidence in love by conflating it with mere *self*-confidence, which he knows she always, no matter how powerful and successful she is, possesses less of than he does. If he is particularly low he will play on her fears of being unloved and abandoned.

Woman's first great weakness is an addiction to material security. Often she is unconscious of this. The most unconscious woman will gravitate to whatever can assuage her fear of uncertainty, be it an individual or an institution. Only the experience of love in her body can give her real security, but she forgets this.

Woman's second great weakness is a refusal to acknowledge her own helplessness. She has no defences against being corrupted by man, and by his world. This is one reason why she needs a man to protect her—to protect her against his world and to protect her against his diabolical self.[12]

Woman thus see-saws between two kinds of men; cowards and bastards. Half the time she is addicted to the niceness and security of cowards, whom she can push around. The other half she is prey to the charm and confidence of bastards, who push her around. Neither cowards nor bastards can reach her heart.[13]

Only love works. Not the personal, selfish, sentimental 'love' of the outer world, but the presence, integrity and passion of the inner truth. Only this can touch a real woman, not 'good looks,' not money and power, not anything that can be added to from the outside. And certainly not effort, persuasion or argument.

You'll find, man, that it's really best not to argue with woman. She will, most likely, take what you say personally. This is one reason why, in our world, which is increasingly run by the personalities[14] of women (or by feminine minds), it has become so difficult to make impersonal criticisms of each other. Everything has become personal.

Women—particularly characterless women—find it very difficult to stand back from a feeling of being criticised ('*I am being attacked!*'). They then respond to the emotion that the criticism produces in their bodies, calling on whatever facts, no matter how remote from the matter at hand, they need in order to dispose of it.

This is one reason—aside from the difficulty they have being consistent and decisive—why women tend to make poor bosses and judges. Just as she finds it extremely difficult (sometimes even painful) to take an argument impersonally, so she has difficulty taking a case impersonally and ruling with dispassion.

Characterless men blow up if a hint of personal criticism reaches their ears. As Fyodor Dostoevsky realised,[15] the more someone lies to themselves, the more easily offended they are—and most people are continually lying to themselves. (I am speaking here of abstract debate, not personal slight).

Man tends to take impersonal criticism as a game, as something essentially separate from his self. Generally speaking, to criticise a man one must best him in argumentative combat, which, combined with the greater insensitivity of men, is why it is proper, not to mention funnier, to aim harsher blows at him.

Although perhaps 'harsher' is not quite the right word here; more *blatant* might be better. For male morality usually comes down to 'overcome evil in overt battle', while female morality is best expressed as 'overcome evil in covert battle'. It is very often unmanly to be nice and gentle with problematic males.

Here we come to another way that feminism has betrayed women. As Hollywood films constantly remind us, the picaresque 'HEROINE'S JOURNEY' is now sexist. Woman must fight openly, and make tough moral choices, in order to become the *hero*. But this is not her nature. She is made to avoid all this male nonsense (nonsense for her that is).

Returning to institutions run by women. Another problem with them is that conservative behaviour tends to predominate. This is because women are less willing to take risks than men and so tend to form structures that reward safety, bureaucracy, proceduralism and attitudes that reward conformity to the status quo.[16]

A third consequence of institutions being directed by female priorities is that fewer people within them strive. There is less aspiration, so greatness is rarer. Defensive mediocrity prevails and superb quality, along with the male competitiveness[17] that greatness requires, is ignored, excluded or punished.

Women thus create and sustain what we understand as 'WOKE' institutions, in which overt striving, along with the harsh argument and criticism such striving demands, are punished, in which 'inclusivity' and 'compassion' take precedence over freedom and excellence, and in which the anxieties of egoic women are pandered to.

This is why we find ourselves in a cultural world which does not threaten women; no biting satire, no obsessive excellence, no sublime tragedy and no male charm. Instead; body-horror, denigration of genius, strong-faced, sexless, heroines, bland sappy heroes, and the soporific, shades-of-beige reassurance of the known.

It is also why 'rape' now largely means (in the unofficial dictionary of identity politics) 'sex I regret',[18] while 'sexual harassment' means 'an approach from a man I am not attracted to'. That such definitions have the force of law behind them is one reason (along with spiritual emasculation), men no longer approach women.

Or take 'toxic masculinity', which really just means 'masculinity' for the pomo left. 'Toxicity' serves a similar function to 'mental illness', in that it makes unpleasant behaviour an institutional concern. It's no longer my responsibility to deal with an arsehole, or his, but a matter for teachers, lawyers and doctors.

Notice that men who are *not* sufficiently masculine, are either ignored for their receding jaws, narrow-shoulders, 'small-dick energy' and so on—or even mocked for such traits—while those who are strong, healthy and decisive are 'toxic'. The message today is, if you are a man—particularly an older man—you cannot win.

Notice also that there is no such thing as 'toxic femininity'. That women (unconscious women I mean) *like* being sex objects, that they *want* to be commodified, that they run, open armed, *towards* socially approved forms of prostitution, that they go out of their minds if they are 'left on the shelf'... all this is heinous wrongthink.

And because it is unsayable, so is the solution. Women cannot free themselves from a situation that it is impossible to openly acknowledge. They can never regulate their sexuality if it is not seen as a problem, nor recognise their need to be loved if they cannot see how being loved resembles being merely desired.

Love is the solution. Love is the ineffable meeting point between essentially complementary differences, which is why it is feared by pseudo-gendered caricatures *and* mono-gendered cyphers, both of whom egoically seek their own reflection (either exaggeratedly sexed or exaggeratedly unsexed) in the beloved.

Love in the world must be made, which is to say brought into the world through and between two complementary opposites. This is the primary purpose of loving sex. Without this purpose, sex becomes mere pleasure, which degrades into either drippy sentimentality or hollow, demonic PORNOGRAPHY.

Porn is a male invention. Woman does not need pornography, because her sexuality is essentially *embodied*, and therefore fundamentally opaque to mind. Man's diabolic *disembodied* need to fuck an idea[19] is one of the principal barriers between him and his woman, the overcoming of which is the secondary purpose of loving sex.[20]

Pornography intensifies the effects of living in a high-tech senile-capitalist system, which itself is pornographic, titillating consumers with long build ups to snowflake orgasms.[21] Pornography speaks to sentiment and expectation, manufacturing anxieties for which the system then proffers palliatives.

The effect on man of consuming pornography is as disastrous as it is on woman. It drains him of vitality, replaces reality with a monstrous idol and slowly turns him into an anaesthetised cypher, a helpless, drained, hungry ghost. He even begins to look like a ghost, like a featureless smudge, not really quite here.

Pornography for man has same source as HOMOSEXUALITY, a hyper-civilised need to seek substitutes for the love of woman, which is beyond him. The male ego turns to his games, to his work, and to his mates, he masturbates, he numbs himself with drugs or he chooses to be gay, which is to say, to assume an *identity* of gayness.

Gay men are afraid of loving women, an unconscious fear they translate into lack of desire for them.[22] There is no such thing as *fundamental* gayness in nature or in natural people. Instances of [unproblematic[23]] gay sex, or occasional same-sex pairs, do not indicate *fundamental* gayness in children, in primal people or in mallard ducks.

Gay and lesbian relationships are common among CYPHERS, which is to say, disembodied, and therefore disgendered men and women. Homosexuality appears in groups that have detached themselves from embodied, functional existence. In the past, superfluous elites and intellectuals, today, urban lefties and liberals.

Cyphers appear when society turns natural growth on its head. The cyphered man refuses to become 'the other', while the cyphered woman is forced to do so. He becomes pathologically embodied, while she becomes pathologically disembodied. This self-obsession starts before desire reaches the threshold of awareness.[24]

The opposame to the asexual cypher is the exaggeratedly sexual CARICATURE, a walking talking reproductive organ whose only real task in life is to spread its genes, with everything they think or do directed towards this one aim. They are equipped with very small brains in order to help them achieve this simple task.

Cyphers (who, as we shall see, are often found on the political left) and caricatures (more common on the right) make a lot of fuss about how different they are from each other, and how right and noble their sexual urges (or lack thereof) are; but they are all unhappy, their lives filled with the same anxiety and contention.

The caricatured, patriarchal 'man's man' is, like the gay man, also afraid of loving women, but he translates his fear into either the promiscuous desire of the bastard, one conquest after another, or the weak surrender of the coward, giving in to the tyrannous emotions of a 'strong' (but bitterly unhappy) mother-wife.

Our loveless, bodiless world thus creates extremely unattractive men; vain, weak, incompetent, unsure, unable to make decisions, unable to take care of themselves without a woman and unable to understand that a short, fat, bald and ugly man with integrity who *can* do these things is more attractive to her than a ripped prince.

Man must resolve the split he was born with. He must learn, from woman, how to plunge into the innocent heart of things, and he must learn, from men, how to master his tools (not his machines, his *tools*, which includes the tool of his own self). Only this way can he stand alone and stand firm. Only this way can women love him.

But man must also learn to commit to one woman. Only through such commitment, and through overcoming his egoic need to get away from her love, can he discover the courage and the presence to master her emotions— in order to overcome his sexual restlessness (masquerading as anger, sexual indifference and wealth-gathering).

A ritualised promise of commitment is, as we shall see, the purpose of marriage. This is why men and women who love each other marry,[25] and this is why it feels nobler to speak of 'my wife' or 'my husband' than to speak of 'my boyfriend' or 'my girlfriend'. Women usually understand this better than men.

Women today in the West[26] often reject love and marriage. They have not really been loved, only wanted, needed, sexually desired and pathetically worshipped. Fawning attention might appeal to the vanity of woman, and she might make use of it to get what she wants, but this kind of 'love' disgusts her.[27]

A woman who is loved is content with poverty.[28] A woman who is loved is not fiendishly jealous, nor is she needy. A woman who is loved will even enjoy being told what to do by a man (indeed she may *love* to be told what to do).[29] A woman who is loved can read this book without losing her fucking mind.

A woman who is not loved will seek *substitutes*, such as having children, career success, cute animals, consumption, moral crusading, chasing youthfulness, endless dramatic chatter and homosexual attention. If woman reaches menopause without having loved and been loved, she'll turn into a sentimental pity monster[30] or a witch.

If she has loved and been loved, a woman at menopause loses her personality, and her love becomes impersonal. This is a very difficult and painful transition, but a woman who has been loved welcomes it. She knows that the depth of the love now dawning in her is roughly that of the entire universe.

There are very few impersonal old women, or wise old men, and the link between those who still exist and the young has been severed by 'youth culture' and social media—i.e. by TECHNOLOGY—leading to a breakdown of culture and a consequent inability of the young to learn the reality of gender from their elders.

Technology has catastrophically fused the private domain of woman with the public domain of man, forcing them to unnaturally compete with each other in a power struggle that did not afflict pre-civilised societies which, despite their problems, were the most sexually egalitarian that have ever existed.

There certainly was appalling male violence towards women in pre-industrial and pre-civilised societies, but there was also, in the separation of domain that all pre-modern peoples took for granted, a degree of protection in the fact that men had their tools, their language, their places of power, and women had theirs.

Pre-modern man could walk into a woman's domain and start ordering her around in her own world, but his power to subjugate and control her there was limited, compared to how he was able to completely dominate her when she was forced, first of all, onto the high-tech factory floor, and then into the high-tech suburban home.

Technology, in the form of various 'labour-saving devices,' and opportunities for social advancement for a lucky few, appeared to free woman from industrial slavery (and from being tied to the SHADOW-WORK[31] of cooking, cleaning and child-care), but at the catastrophic cost of severing male and female COMPLEMENTARITY entirely.

For as woman entered the male world, she lost more than her dignity. She also lost her *difference*. The strange magic of two different creatures coming together, in love, was then impossible. Henceforth, friendly compatibility, mutual respect and shared economic goals would occupy the place where love used to be.

The final frontier for the technological system is the sexed body itself. This body, for those who serve the system, is not a natural *reality* that humans are born with, and that permits the complementarity of gendered difference, but a *limitation* to be overcome so that humans might free themselves completely from sex and gender.

This 'transhuman' dystopia, promoted by radical theorists such as Judith Butler, will never come to pass, but the formation of a technological society that is conducive to it is already here, and is already corrupting the embodied sexuality of young people, who find themselves tragically alienated from their own bodies.

Technology has thus led to a total breakdown of natural gendered relations. The sexual league table, for example, once a *locality* that character, spirit and love could all find a place on, has been warped by the screen into a crude global *arena* of a few winners, who get all the attention, and a mass of losers and outcasts.

Women at the top of the sexual league table sometimes affect to be exhausted by the 'toxic masculinity' of men who harass them, but most of these 'beautiful' women are addicted to the attention the world gives them, which is why they are invariably the most bored and boring (not to mention tragically unsensuous) of creatures.

Some young women are too weak or too sensitive to handle predatory attention from men and actually seek to be ugly or invisible. They cultivate ugliness for much the same reason as sexual losers do, because it gives them an excuse to not have to make an effort to handle men, which they are quite capable of doing.

Some people who are not desired are simply demoralised. Everyone wants to be loved for their appearance, because everyone knows that appearance and essence are not separate entities. The simplest solution, in a world with unrealistic standards of formal 'beauty', is to refuse to play the game at all.

Other losers in the sexual league exult in their status as outcasts. These are invariably the laziest and most mediocre of perma-children, manufactured today by the world in their millions, although most are invisible because they spend their lives glued to the sexless screen, which they call 'the real world'.

This 'real world' indeed mirrors the sexless screen, which is how sex and gender—their character, difference and complementarity—have become effaced, and why it has become sacrilegious to speak of their difference. But speak we must, even if it makes us outcasts, for a body without distinction is a corpse.

Speaking of Love

The word 'love' sounds cheesy, like hearts and flowers.[1] To speak of love literally is to manufacture cliché and invite a cynical shrug. Love, like consciousness, quality and truth, is not a literal thing, and so it is impossible to speak of it literally without betraying it. This is one reason why it is so difficult to say 'I love you'.

And it's why to say things like 'God is love' or 'love is truth' or to present logical arguments for the existence or quality of such things, is to expose oneself to irrefutable rational objection ('prove it!') and invite either boredom ('I am not interested') or sycophancy ('Oh wow, that's *so* interesting!').

The only way to speak of love truthfully is indirectly, non-literally and non-spatially; to present it in terms of what it is like (which we call METAPHOR), what it is not (which goes by the name of APOPHASIS) and through the musical rhythm and poetry of language, particularly in live, spoken language (which we call TONE).

Such truthful speech is not something that can be learnt in the normal way. You can learn the literal meaning of words, but you cannot learn what they metaphorically, apophatically and tonally have in common, because you are that. It is not knowledge that produces meaning but consciousness, and consciousness precedes knowledge.

This is why whatever it is you know about love ends up causing you pain. You have learnt it is such-and-such a person, such-and-such an experience, but then it appears as an entirely different person and experience, and so it either passes you by, or you destroy it by trying to force it into your preconceptions.

The mystery of consciousness also explains how very clever people can be such cretins in matters of real importance—when facing situations which do not demand knowledge, but an ability to act without knowledge[2]—and how young children, who know next to nothing, can be wiser (not to mention more courageous) than professors.

This is why philosophers, those people whom we would hope could help us understand love, either avoid the subject altogether or write about it superficially. They offer few insights into love, certainly none that are useful, because they only *know* what love is. They cannot speak from direct experience of love, because they have none.[3]

Professional thinkers are confused about the reality of love because it comes before any thought or verbal expression of it. It must be here, in this room, before I can speak of it, and before you can hear it. If you merely know what I am talking about, it is not love you are reading about, but your idea of it.

It may be true that love is sleeping in you, that, although my words are coming to you confusedly, as if from a dream, they touch something true inside. If that is the case, this book will seem 'interesting' to you, but in all likelihood the most important points will pass you by and you will soon forget the rest.

Or you might have very little love in you at all, and can only attend to the state through the prism of your self, which makes anything sweeter or stranger than thought or emotion seem boring, stupid or a form of evil.[4] But if that were the case, you would not have read this far, unless you're reading in order to attack me, or to attack love.

Or you may be in love, right now, happy today with the beauty of it; then there's hardly any reason to read at all, except to enjoy the pleasure of recognition. This is why lovers enjoy being in nature, because nature reflects the simplicity, the beauty and the wonderful vitality of being in love.

The World's War on Love

So what is love? Where is it to be found? Not in the world. Everywhere in the world one encounters the sentimental image of love, the exciting advertisement of it and the fascinating idea of it, but never the direct experience of it, here in the body. This is because the loveless world that we live in—and as—fears and hates love.

The world fears and hates the INCARNATION of love (from the Latin *incarnare*, 'into the flesh'), it fears and hates the SACRIFICE[1] of love (from the Latin *sacer*, 'holy') and it fears and hates the PASSION of love (from the Latin *passionem*, 'suffer'), because incarnation, sacrifice and passion threaten the self upon which society is constructed.

It is impossible to be incarnated in the world (as every woman knows). You cannot be allow the body to feel (i.e. to be SENSITIVE) nor to act (to be SPONTANEOUS). The body must be controlled and its instincts redirected through the polite rational mind, which is why civilisation has waged war on the body millennia.

Sacrifice is also impossible, as is the mysterious, non-institutional spirit that sacrifice is for. Only what is *definable, material*[2] and *useful* is of value in the world. To give that up in favour of something indefinable, immaterial and useless is to incite, at best, incomprehension and, at worst, active persecution.[3]

And passion? It is nowhere to be found. Not in the classroom, not in the office, not in the factory, not on the farm. One finds an imitation of passion—emotional emphasis, effort, desperate browbeating and desire—but the passion that comes from the abnegation or overcoming of self is as rare as the love which inspires it.

Until recently we allowed a few entertainers to experience and express the incarnation, sacrifice and passion of love, particularly musicians, because mere entertainers have no material influence on the world, on the nitty-gritty *business* of getting things done, and so they can be safely ignored, like clowns.

And if they cannot be ignored, they must be dealt with. A little bit of pressure goes a long way with writers and artists, but fame alone is enough to uproot the loving heart, which is why fame inevitably destroys creativity and why, in our world, in which everyone is a little bit famous, there is no love to suppress.

All this explains why there is so much CYNICISM about love. The simple fact is that very few people ever encounter love, and when they do (for, in reality, it is everywhere), they are incapable of recognising it. When someone speaks of 'love' they might as well be speaking of Father Christmas or the Tooth Fairy.[4]

The number of people in the world who know what real love is, or who have made real love is minute. This is why people don't like to talk about their sex lives, except indirectly, jokingly, boastfully (usually men), or with a fake sentimental gloss (usually women), because their love lives are a source of boredom, confusion and shame.

For just as society fears and hates the incarnation, sacrifice and passion of love, so do the selves that comprise society, who are so conditioned by society to fit into its needs that they are incapable of sensing their body from within, giving up their desires and fears (or their likes and dislikes) and feeling the joy of love.

And so the world appears to us as it does; an unreal, selfish and passionless land of misery, frustration, irritation, indifference, boredom, anxiety and anger; constant loveless emotionality relieved for a few giddy moments on holiday, in the pub, before the screen or at the point of orgasm. This is 'normal'.

And it has always been so. The fear that today's society has of gendered sexuality, of man and woman overcoming the boundaries of the dissolute modern self, appears to be quite different to pre-modern prudishness and the persecution of sex outside of socially acceptable marriage, but they are the same.

The clue is in the word 'boundary'. The locus of social law has been transferred from the repressive *institution* to the repressed *self*, both of which are threatened by incarnation, sacrifice and passion, which is to say by love, which is mercilessly punished in selfish institutions *and* in institutionalised selves.

In the past, the institution—first the state, the court and the church, then the school, the hospital and the corporation—puritanically controlled sexuality. Today, the self is neutered by its fusion with the sexless machine, and so errant sexuality does not need to be punitively disciplined, for the self manages itself.

The neutered self is neutral; it has no passional need for anything, much less its gendered opposite. It is a GREY SALMON, alive but senescent, content to decay in its little pool. This meets the needs of the technological system, which prefers herds of fungible, docile human units over recalcitrant and passionate individuals, very well.

(Grey salmon also meet the needs of fearful, egoic women—mothers who cannot bear to push their little boys into the hands of men, and feminist professionals who cannot bear to submit to male intelligence and power. Such women, by gelding men and suppressing maleness, do the work of the technological system.)

Modern society does not, therefore, punish man and woman for illegal or immoral sexual acts (gay sex, infidelity, promiscuity, prostitution, pornography, etc.) but for passionate, gendered sexuality *itself*. The late capitalist system is not interested in managing you, but in ensuring you do not need to be managed.

Even innocuous expressions of sexuality, such as a man admiring a woman, are today construed as unforgivable sexual violence, or, conversely, if a woman submits to male attention, as shameful complicity. A man taking control of a situation, and a woman gladly submitting to such control, is beyond the pale.

In the past, it required great courage to get divorced, to love someone of the same sex, to have two partners, to exhibit your body or to be androgynous. Today, it requires great courage to stay married, to love someone of the opposite sex, to be monogamous and, above all, to be a real man, or a real woman.[5]

Free sexuality is thus punished everywhere and at all times. Theocracies and monarchies, leftist and rightist states, feudal lords and corporate managers. The war on the body merely changes its form, just as its priests change their costumes, but they all police love with the same hysterical intolerance.

The pendulum swings back and forth, from exhibitionism to excessive modesty, from right-wing suppression to left-wing license. Sooner or later it will swing again, and garish sexuality will be everywhere, prudery will be scorned, and nothing will have changed for love, which simply dies a different kind of death.

But not for the conscious man and woman. Only he or she can discover the incarnate sacrifice and passion needed to overcome the heartless cancer of the world, whether that world takes the form of rabidly self-assertive, licentious individualism or of masochistically self-abnegating, puritanical collectivism.

Only the conscious man or woman can make love, and only making love can save them from the world, not just the brutally uncaring world of selves outside, but the selfish inner world of emotion, of anguished wanting and worrying, that the loveless self hauls through the day like a bag of vipers.

Attachment and Resistance

To love and to make love you must already be in love. Not, first of all, with your partner, and certainly not with your self—which will take all the love you can ever give it and still want more—but with life. If life doesn't come first, your love will be *conditional*, which will make it needy, greedy and laced with anxiety.

'But there is nothing I can love!' To offer such a complaint more or less guarantees that you cannot make love with anything but your own misery. If you can find nothing to love, or be grateful for, in your life now, you'll grasp at love when it comes along later, and then, like a shadow, it will slip away.

You cannot make love if you have no love to give, and you have no love to give if you are not giving it now. Love isn't capital, it's not a substance which sits in the warehouse of the soul, waiting for the right person to come along and order it. Love is the experience of giving itself, over and over and over again.

What can you give your love to? Obviously, *first of all*, the room you are in (including the room of the body). It might be an ugly room, and there might be pain in it, but unlike any other room in the universe, it is an actual room. You can only love, or be grateful for, what is actual. Anything else is sentiment and belief.

Secondly, following love for the bare existence of what is, there are parts of what is. Reading these words is lovely, isn't it? (If it's not, for God's sake go and do something that is). What about the pleasure of being able to breathe freely? Or of sharing your life with someone you love? Or of having a roof, hot water and food?

No? You can't find *anything* to love, now? The sky through the window? Someone who cares for you in your family? Your cat? Your good health? The warmth of your underwear? Your roof? Your youth? Your experience? Or just the pleasure of being you? Nothing at all? Well then, you cannot love. Be off with you. Read a different book.

CONSCIOUS ATTENTION on what you love—above all on bare existence—is not CONCENTRATION though. It is not 'tight focus', there's no effort about it, no trying. You cannot try to love—trying frustrates and disappoints. Conscious attention is soft and easy. There is, ultimately, just a lovely inward sensation, that makes you smile slightly.

This means that conscious attention is necessarily, ultimately, SELFLESS. There may be separate things your self loves—your friends, your car, your books—but the sensation of love that precedes them is necessarily selfless. There is no personal choice about it, no wanting or not-wanting. It's just what is.[1]

If bare selfless attention doesn't come first, it will be the self that is deciding, or trying to decide what to want and what to do, and as the self is inherently self-ish, and incapable of perceiving the present moment, all action that comes from its perceptions and conceptions will be confused and lead to regret.

What happens is that the loveless self focuses on secondary things, which, without the bare ground of love, become ATTACHMENTS. I get attached to the secondary things of my life, and start wanting and needing them. This makes me wanty and needy, which, as we all know, is not love at all, but the betrayal of it.

Attachment is very easy to distinguish from love; it comes with anxiety about losing its object, because it depends on that object—that person—for its nice, up feelings. Then, when that object leaves, or breaks, or is taken away (as all objects and people do—*all* of them), I suffer. I am heart-broken. 'Oh,' I cry, 'where has my love gone?'

Idiot. It wasn't love at all. This is why, as you'll notice both from your own disastrous choices of partner and from those of the people around you, there is so much regret in the world, because the loveless *self* is looking for love, and the loveless *self* is choosing who to love,[2] which always leads to shame, disappointment and regret.

And this is why there is no ANSWER to the problem of love. Answers are based on *things* the self has learnt about love, from artists, from priests, from scientists and from friends and family. These people may have been in love (unlikely), but your knowledge of what they teach is not rich, living love, it is the past, implanted in you.

The first people to implant the unhappy past in you were your parents. It was your mother and father who formed the deepest foundation for your preconceptions about love. Not through what they merely taught you—that comes later—but from the quality of their attention which, when you were very young, was your reality entire.

Most parents are loving, to some degree, but their loving attention is corrupted by EMOTION—irritation, anxiety, depression—which cuts them off from the situation and therefore from their children, who thereby find themselves isolated, alone and in enemy territory. This is why so many young children cry 'for no reason'.

The existentially isolated child, alone and in enemy territory, then becomes emotional itself. Because it does not feel the existential nourishment of loving attention, it either withdraws into itself completely, and becomes a kind of numb nothing or, more commonly, it begins to *demand* attention. It acts up.

None of this is conscious. The child is not *trying* to get its parents worked up, exasperated or angry. It is possessed by unhappy, unconscious emotion which can do nothing but perpetuate itself, by exciting itself and exciting others. It doesn't think about the consequences, which are always painful.

And it still does this, in the adult. Emotion cannot rest in stillness and ease. The moment is never sufficient unto itself. It must seek excitement. Some people look for excitement in drugs, some in violence (passively enjoying it, or actively provoking it others), some in sex, some in attention, some in food, and some in all of these things.

But the form of addictive excitement (or FUN) stems from childhood, when you first learnt to deal with the pain of emotion. It was then that you learnt to be bad, or to hanker for attention (perhaps by being 'good'), or to stuff your face with sweets, or to descend into an inner world of daydreams and fantasies.

Bad then becomes evil, attention becomes sexual attention,[3] being 'good' becomes servility, being naughty becomes cruelty, sweets become drugs and an inner world of fantasy becomes a tomb world of anaesthetised nothingness. The details change, from person to person, but the same sorry story is repeated everywhere.

And this is one reason[4] it feels so 'good' to be bad. Having a hundred thousand men drool over your naked body, or getting smashed every night, or slavishly working yourself into the grave, such insanity feels 'good' because it feels *comfortable*, the comfort you learnt to find when you were very young.

Another example of this is unconscious desire for a reflection of one's opposite-sex parent. When, for example, a man whose mother was ambitious and manipulative meets an ambitious, manipulative woman he senses that here is the home he always needed. Their 'love' will be horribly painful, but again it feels 'good'.

One's parents, and particularly one's mother, represent the entire human universe to the child, who then grows up and goes out into the world feeling uncomfortable in any other kind of universe (particularly, today, any kind of *male* universe[5]), no matter how loving, intelligent, wise or giving.

Attachment and Resistance

You acquired, from your parents, emotional pain and the means by which the self attempts to deal with that pain; RESISTANCE. In fact, self is resistance (or form), but this 'systolic' resistance should naturally, 'diastolically', relax back into the formless situation, into the selfless moment or context.

Where there is constant emotion in the situation, self cannot relax. It is in a state of perpetual tension. This manifests physically, as stiffness or up-tightness of feature, of gait or of tone of voice. It leads to the hard, heavy, inflexibly mask-like face and squeezed, awkward speech of the repressed and unhappy man or woman.

But even the sweetest and most loving face and body will harden under the pressure of pain. If you are conscious, you will feel this in others, and if you are very conscious you'll sense it in your self. The softness and ease has gone, and in its place is a clench, and the name of this clench is emotion.

Some people are literally twisted up with emotion. For others, emotion presses down like a sad weight on their chests. For some, emotion is a vice that squeezes the neck, making the voice sound tight and tuneless. Or emotion might manifest as constant simmering bile, or a sense of outrage, ready to lash out at the slightest challenge.

Emotion of course cannot see things this way. Emotion will call itself truth and love, but it is neither. It is warlike desire and fear of being alone. Emotion is the living past, appearing as the problematic condition of the present. If you are unable to overcome emotion, you cannot perceive the present, which means you cannot love.

Thus, the foundation of love between two people is supreme, emotionless aloneness, now. If you cannot live alone in the present, without relying on props, such as imagination, fantasy, hope and narcotic stimulation or suppression (including the narcotic of the screen), then you can never love. And you will die unfulfilled.

Sex and Getting Off

I am using the word SEX in a special and limited sense in this book; to mean *loveless* fucking; *unconscious* intercourse. Conscious intercourse, by contrast, is referred to in this book as LOVEMAKING, but the terms are not so important. You can use whatever words you like, provided you can perceive the distinction I am making here.

Sex is motivated by *selfish* emotion, mental-emotional wanting laced with mental-emotional fear of not getting. Sex is selfish because it is what the self, cut off from the moment, thinks and feels it needs to *get*. It is impossible to feel this need if you are selflessly experiencing the present moment, because you must *give* your self to do so.

Sexually restless men and women are not *givers*. They might hand over money, attention or gratification; they might seem to be *ever* so nice. But when it comes down to it, they are essentially *getters* and *takers*, because they are essentially selfish, trapped in the self, and so only able to experience pleasure within the self.

This is why caged animals masturbate so much, and why man, caged in his self, and in the prison of his self-made society, consumes pornography, an idea of sex, of something to get, projected onto the screen of his mind. Woman, more selfless, does not have this desperate need, which is why, naturally, she is more loving and giving.

Woman has a lower sexual temperature than man, partly because of her lack of testosterone and her need to be selective in choosing a mate, but she is also more present than man, and so less in love with conceptual fantasy. Her fantasies are emotional, although they are soon shattered on the hard reality of her experience.

A young woman may lack presence, and require a lifetime to return to the source of love, the body that man's world makes an alien object of, and she may be given to absurd dreams of what love can be, but, at least potentially, she is far closer to the reality of love than young men, who are children in comparison.

But then she has sex with a man, an extremely disappointing experience, even if the horrors of the pornographic screen have steeled her to the reality of man's sexuality. If it is unlikely that she encounters a man who 'knows what to do' with her body, it is almost impossible that she comes across one who can reach her heart.

So she joins him in sex. Sex is a private experience, lights out, eyes closed, heart closed, FUCKING. He leaves first, enjoying the tremendously exciting pornographic idea of what is happening, and then she, unwilling to be left alone out in the cold, withdraws into her world, enjoying the feeling of being enjoyed.

Fucking can be very pleasurable—it rarely is, but it certainly can be. But such pleasure is not happiness, not joy, not delight, which is why it is possible to have 'good sex' without a hint of happiness, joy or delight.[1] In reality, pleasure more intense than you can imagine is a *by-product* of happiness, joy and delight.

Notice how you feel about those words, happiness, joy and delight. Because they cannot be spoken of directly, only experienced (and then, as we've seen, only expressed indirectly, through metaphor), they almost certainly evoke an idea, and therefore either sentimental interest or cynical disinterest in the idea.

Generally speaking then, man gets off on having woman, and she gets off on being had—he is inclined to SADISM and she to MASOCHISM—but there is a vast range of specific variations, which today we call KINKS, although in the past they were known, more correctly, as PERVERSIONS.

Two Kinds of Perversion

Perversions are both social and personal. Socially, they are transgressive, or TABOO, in that the pleasure of them comes from a self-assertive violation of social boundaries or TOTEMS. As such, they can be seen as parodies of freedom, the kind that children enjoy in being naughty simply for the self-satisfying sake of it.

Today in the West there are two fundamental social perversions; that of the management class, whose totem is EQUALITY—and whose taboo is therefore the transgressive sub-dom power-play of BDSM—and that of the elite class, whose totem is TRADITION—and whose taboo is therefore infidelity, voyeurism and multi-partner sex.

Although taboos demonstrate the existence of totems, they also serve to regulate and reinforce them. Infidelity serves as a pressure valve for stultifying monogamy and BDSM and similar such 'transgressive practices' serve as a release from the pressure of maintaining the religion of fairness and inclusion.[1]

Personal perversions tend not to be TRANSGRESSIVE (*against* the social other) but EXCESSIVE (*for* the personal self). The self enjoys itself and seeks, in sex, a symbolic reflection of its singularity, of its particular combination of modalities, and its particular desires, for this or that person, this or that quality.

If self is in its place, perversions, like phobias, remain innocuous, trivial and, as it were, disposable. A man might like submissives who'll wear bunny ears, a woman might like strong hairy men who can easily pick her up, and each will tend to go for someone who approaches his or her modal reflection. And what's wrong with that?

Two Kinds of Perversion

Nothing. There is nothing wrong with 'being a pervert' in this sense, which is a manifestation of strong, healthy, sexual desire. In this sense it is vitally important that you *are* a pervert, that you *are* horny; that you *do* 'lust' after beautiful creatures. You are a sexual, gendered *animal* and so-called asexuality is a betrayal of that.

Or is almost certainly a betrayal of that. I am using ASEXUAL in this book to refer to the numbed, genderless, passionless state of postmodernity. In fact, as outlined in the first two chapters, there are people in the world who are naturally *less* sensuous than others, whose sexuality is more ambiguous, or perhaps more 'delicate'.

The problem is that the selfish self, unable to reach beyond itself in love, is either *dead* to sex or *obsessed* with it. Unable to selflessly rest in its own conscious centre, it is numb to passion or desperate to conquer or be conquered, which leads to what was once called the sin of lust, and what here I am calling perversion in a negative sense.

The unconscious, sex-mad self, not content with the simplicity of love and the simple body of the other, *needs* perverse, fetishised excess, an array of PROPS and the use of TECHNIQUE in order to stimulate itself. These become more exaggerated over time, as the self ages, or as the excitement of sexual conquest wears off.

The end result, found most often in older men, is sexual DEVIANCY—rape (actual rape, that is), murder and child abuse—the terminus of the sexual self, considered by advocates of kink to be a radically different order of experience to perversion, and not, as it actually is, ordinary sexual excitement taken to its gruesome extreme.

Sex *is* gruesome excitement, an image of an end, a result that the restless, unhappy self projects upon the other and then pursues *to* that end—to the fabled orgasm. Post-coital rest doesn't last very long though. It's soon desperate again, for another end, and then another, and then another, *ad infinitum, ad dolorum, ad mortem.*

The body is never excited. It has no need for an end, and therefore no need for sex. In its selfless simplicity the body loves and admires the earth, or the earthy female form, or a lovely work of art, but it has no need to *get* these things, to dominate or be dominated by them, and feels no regret that they have slipped through its fingers.

This is one reason why, throughout history, man has been so desperate to control the body—particularly the bodies of women and children—and hide it from view; because he fears and hates the simplicity, spontaneity and mysterious actuality of the body, and because he cannot free himself of his agonising craving to get at it.

This craving is SUFFERING. The body may feel PAIN, sometimes horrendous pain, but it never suffers. Suffering is the self's judgement of pain, its fear of pain, its hatred of pain, its whining straining away from pain and its addiction to analgesics, including the most potent analgesic of all, the orgasm.

The self's never-ending thirst for orgasm (along with the various substitutes for orgasm that the world offers to those unable to pursue sexual release) is never-ending suffering. It is suffering in the pursuit, and as all who know who've lain in misery after lovelessly ejaculating into another, it is suffering in the outcome.

The identity of sex and suffering is evident in the sexual nature of sadism and masochism, and in the sado-masochistic nature of loveless fucking. Weak or passive egos long to be dominated and abused; strong or active egos long to dominate and abuse (although selves, being a composite of modalities, can comprise both poles).

The vicious circle of sex—disinterest, desperation, excess, satisfaction, sated disinterest—along with the various substitutes which stand in for sex—wealth-gathering, consumption, screen addiction, violent films, video games, spectator sport and more literal forms of porn—comprises life in the world.

The World is Fucked

The world then is composed of selves which cannot understand love, only understand sex and its substitutes and surrogates; sport, business, politics, war, fame, narcotics, the screen and, insofar as it is used to avoid love, the family, all of which compensate man for being a selfish, inept lover, and woman for being lonely, bored and unloved.

A desire to fuck and be fucked powers all the sadism and masochism, and all the inhuman ideologies, myths and practices that violent fear and fearful violence lead to. Sex is behind all violence towards women and children and sex powers the greed that leads to violence towards all people, especially the poor.

Thus, rampant sexuality suits the technological system just fine. Without restless emotional craving, the commodification of the gendered soul and the deification of sexualised youth, the machine would fall apart. It needs fresh, sellable young things that ardently desire sexualised attention to learn its skills and fetishise its output.

Consider advertising. Until recently it was almost unthinkable to try and sell a car without a youthful pair of breasts jiggling about in front of it; to want the youthful, highly-sexualised body is to want the sexualised product. Sex sells; not love, sex. You cannot advertise a product with love, because love reduces wanting.

Or consider the world's worship of youth. This is because a machine-world demands fungible young things, full of energy and able to adapt to today's technological requirements. This is why everywhere we turn, on every surface, we see young flesh beaming back at us, laughing, happy and in fraternal accord.

The end result of technological progress however, is not sexual pleasure, but asexual NUMBNESS. Man's mission to dominate nature terminates in a sexless, spiritually exhausted, solipsistic society of the screen which obliterates demonic sexuality and dystopian desperation but also heavenly sensuality and utopian passion.

Where once the system demanded overt, licentious sexuality, now—motivated by an ideological obsession with machine-friendly equality—it promotes prudish hyper-modesty and the repressive use of ugly, overweight, desexed bodies to promote its products. One no longer consumes from excited desire but from suffocated anxiety.[1]

The society of the screen has created an onmi-pornographic world of shameless perversity, while, at the same time, by relocating the body into the device, it has drained life of sensuality, of flirtatious playfulness and of an innocent 'man-woman thing' which once made social life so agreeable, so adventurous.[2]

Screen dating has stolen woman's intuition and appetite for risk. She must now assess suitors rationally, through disembodied facts (images and 'metrics'). Her embodied sensitivity to the spirit of man plays no part in the screen, preventing the characterful silence, tone and smell of a real man from ever reaching her.

Not that spiritless modern man minds. The screen works in his favour. He is comfortable approaching a woman through the intermediary of data and he is glad that her irksome, cryptic, mystifying femininity, with its outmoded need for chivalry, delicacy, commitment and genius, plays no part in the modern ritual of 'hooking up'.

She goes along with all this because she no longer possesses the sensual presence to respond to masculine character, even if it existed. He is incapable of charming her, and she is incapable of being charmed, so she submits to merely having her boxes ticked. Civilisation is a box-ticking exercise anyway, so it all seems normal.

The World is Fucked

We find ourselves in the utopia of radical feminism, in which woman is free to 'ziplessly fuck' her way through life, without fear of consequence, in which, as in Huxley's Brave New [Feminist, Socialist, Utopian] World, 'everyone belongs to everyone else'. This is also the utopia of the first radical feminist; de Sade.

The Marquis de Sade, an egalitarian, inclusive, tolerant and perfectly rational Enlightenment thinker, believed that 'all men, all women resemble each other'; they are interchangeable objects which must be allowed freedom to pursue their desires, no matter how perverse. His dream has become our reality.[3]

Sade's utopia is also Fay Weldon's, Erica Jong's and Germaine Greer's. These 'second wave feminists' repudiate the monster they have given birth to, sexless, genderless, transsexualism, but our sadistic-narcissistic world is an inevitable consequence of the technocratic 'freedom' they pursued.

Technology gave modern woman the washing machine, which freed her from the sink; it gave her immigrant cleaners, which freed her from the ironing board; it gave her pill, which freed her from pregnancy; it gave her the screen, which freed her from society; and it gave her the surgeon's knife, which freed her from her body.

Oddly though, woman isn't too happy about her freedom. She is lonelier, angrier, more emotional and more unfulfilled than she has ever been. She has lost her love, her power, her presence, her empathy, her mystery, her home, her family and her body. She is now, like the man she has become, nothing.

It is impossible for an unconscious mechanism, such as the technological system, to have a 'purpose', nevertheless it is quite accurate to say, metaphorically, that this, the annihilation of strong sensations, intense feelings and gendered quality, is the end and object of progress.[4] But it wasn't always that way.

Primal and Civilised Love

Originally, or PRIMALLY, sexual love was unitary; neither decent nor indecent, neither sacred nor profane, distinctions which would have been as meaningless to primal man as those between work and play, or between nature and culture. Men and women made extraordinary love, and there was nothing so ordinary.

We can infer this from the sexuality of primal people who, until recently, survived beyond the reach of civilised agriculture, and the dominating consciousness that civilisation brought into the world. They had their problems—above all sexual jealousy—but the perversion and deviance of our world was unknown.

It is a well-attested fact that so-called 'simple' hunter-gatherers exhibited remarkable sexual egalitarianism compared to later agricultural societies, and although coercion and violence were not, despite romantic idealisations, unknown, neither was sexual freedom, lack of sexual shame or absence of psychologically crippling taboos.[1]

The facts of course, are debatable and debated, but although facts must be honoured, we are speaking here of *qualities* which are beyond the reach of anthropology, or indeed of any scientific enquiry. Such qualities are not encoded in stud, but expressed in MYTH; the myth of unitary innocence that is common to all cultures.

When we speak of the garden paradise that man and woman once lived in, we are not principally speaking of a literal place at a literal time—even if something very much like that did exist—but of an original psychological truth, experienced together in the state we call love, that men and women have forgotten.

The origin myth of *our* civilisation—the Garden of Eden—does not reflect this state. It presents a distant, male, tribal God who punishes man and woman for failing a test they cannot pass, and then puts the blame on woman (as well as on her traditional consort, the snake) for all human suffering.

The dismal Jewish myth of Eden, taken up by Christianity and Islam (and even, in a sense, by secular atheism), does not reflect our original state but the endless nightmare of fear and desire that civilised man is heir to, the consequence of a split in the unitary psyche which afflicted mankind around ten thousand years ago.

The rise of civilisation saw the appearance of distinctions that have tossed man hither and yon ever since; play and work, heaven and earth and life and death; all *ultimately* meaningless to primal folk, but for civilians the source of an existential struggle (to avoid death and reach a playful heaven) from which he would never find peace.

This struggle manifested most conspicuously, as a constant battle between PATRIARCHY, the rule of power (which exploited excellence), manifest in the civilised king, priest or philosopher-father, and FRATERNITY, the rule of conformity (which exploited freedom), manifest in the democracy, secret society and philosopher-comrade.

From Plato's academy, through the democratic revolution of early modernity to Marx's brotherhood of man, fraternalism has been in perpetual conflict with the paternalism of the Aristotelian family, the kingly authority of the medieval lord and the financial power of the capitalist chief executive officer.[2]

The name we give to this unbearably unpleasant struggle is HISTORY, a long descent, by a series of downward steps, towards the schizoid hell we live in today, in which everything of value has been cut in two in order to make a few men anxiously happy and everyone else miserably depressed.

By the time the Bronze Age dawned, around five thousand years ago, love had also been cut in two. It was either a holy experience or a profane one. Love had become either *eros*, a kind of sexual insanity, or *philia*, an intellectual meeting of friendly minds.[3] It was no longer an everyday mystery, uniting opposites.[4]

Christianity, which had an even more confused understanding of sexual love, introduced a distinction between eros and *agape*, selfless, unconditional, sacrificial love. In its fanatical desire to elevate bodiless agape to the stars, it then relegated eros to sinful materiality, a consequence of our fallen nature.

In the medieval period, literate Christians, Jews and Muslims—the priestly minority—maintained civilised man's fanatic hostility to woman, sexuality and the body, in strenuous conflict with ordinary people, who continued to have a relatively healthy attitude to erotic love, at least in comparison to the age which followed.[5]

And yet, overt repression, despite its salience, was never, as Michel Foucault taught, the real mechanism of control. The Church did not really silence desire but made it speak endlessly, carving it up into categories of sin to be confessed, scrutinized, and managed; categories handed over to the modern priests of the PROFESSIONAL CLASS.

The new priestly bourgeoisie thus suppressed gendered sexuality not by denying desire, but by pathologising the wrong kind of desire. The same prudishness and condemnatory coercion reign in 'permissive' societies as they do in 'repressive' societies, with overt radicalism used to conceal covert conformity.

Windows of genuine sexual freedom[6] occasionally open up, but these are suppressed by the covertly repressive 'permissive' left *and* by the overtly repressive 'principled' right. Nothing changes for love, any more than anything changes for nature or for the lot of the poor when a polity swings from capitalism to socialism or vice versa.

Emotion and Feeling

The split between heavenly and earthly love introduced by fallen man, and elevated to a pathological mania by Greek, Jewish and Christian theocracies, is created by EMOTION, which is, as we have seen, the principal obstacle to—and illusory mirror of—a love which unites illusory opposites, such as mind and matter.

Emotion is not the same as FEELING (or pure SENSATION), which, unlike emotion, is ultimately selfless in that it is united with the present and partakes of its quality. Emotion is selfish in that, although it blames anything it can for its state, and although it infects everyone around it, it is an essentially *personal* experience.

Emotion separates me from you, this here from that there. My empathic experience of the quality of the moment—its 'aura', 'atmosphere' or 'vibe'—breaks down and is replaced by a self-interested reaction to it, a desire to get something from the situation or a fear of losing something in it.

In reality, the fear and desire are the same, a suffering that one feels (if one feels it at all) as a heaviness in the belly, a weight across the chest, a tightness in the neck and, eventually, a weariness or tension in the head. Ultimately, this suffering has no object; it is the self's experience of itself, cut off from the context.

Emotion cannot bear to see itself this way, as self-generated, because this would entail RESPONSIBILITY and the end of the sovereignty of emotion over consciousness. So emotion *immediately* seizes on an object, something to fear or desire, as the 'reason' it feels unhappy, dissatisfied, stressed, bored, angry or what-have-you.

This 'seizure' is a mechanical process. You'll be feeling fine, then have a thought about something that troubles you, something rather trivial perhaps, and then suddenly there's all this miserable agitation and pain swirling around inside of you, which takes hours, sometimes a day or two, to dissipate.

Where did it come from? As with arguments with your loved one over preposterously unimportant matters, it is not the worry itself which is troubling, and which you may recognise does not *really* bother you, but all the stored emotional pain you're carrying around in you that has suddenly been activated by your thinking self.

Freedom begins not with freedom from problems, which is impossible, but with freedom from *thought*; not complete moronic thoughtlessness, for of course you must use your mind, but freedom from being used *by* your mind, of being thought by *it*, of being a victim of the past it layers up and up in your psyche like a pile of corpses.

But how? How!? How to be free of the tyranny of restless thought and worry? As we have seen, it begins with love, here, in the room you are in; meaning here in the conscious experience of the body, where there is no useless thought, no frantic decision-making, no restless wanting. Only pain, and pain is a teacher.

You must consciously be in the sensation of your body, now, without escaping from the uncanny simplicity of the experience into your memories and desires. You must accept [emotional] pain, without fleeing into thought, into wanting and worrying, and, if the pain is asking you to act, you must be brave enough to do so.

Only this way can you exit the solipsistic prison of your mental-emotional self. The only way out is in. Only the conscious body can access that which is not limited by the spectacle which the self projects onto the screen of my mind. Only the body can love, which is why history has waged war on the body for ten millennia.

Because emotion is personal it cannot, unlike conscious feeling, respond empathically to the inner life of the other and must instead use TECHNIQUE to deal with him or her. As Albert Camus said, when one has no character—which is to say no conscious, empathic feeling of inner quality—'one has to apply method.'

Methods for dealing with the other include emotional manipulation (guilt-tripping, flattery, playing on weaknesses), violence (or implied threats), rational management (which includes relying on the rational management of the system to get one's way with others) and misanthropically avoiding people altogether.

The emotional mind is diabolically clever. It uses your mind to get what it wants, and to hide that it's after something from you and from others. It is a factory of justifications, manufacturing rationalisations and excuses which it sells to other minds in exchange for a tacit agreement to buy the same product in return.

It is not conscious of any of this, except occasionally in the most distant, abstract manner.[1] The emotional mind works mechanically,[2] which means it is threatened by non-mechanical consciousness, which it pushes from its awareness whenever or however it appears; in a moment's silence, for example, or in an uncomfortable truth.

This is how people can behave so selfishly and not appear to feel the slightest remorse; because selfishness and lack of remorse are both consequences of being unconscious. It's also how making people emotional (through stimulating their fears and desires) makes them unconscious, stupid and easy to manipulate.

Because the emotional mind fears and, consequently, hates conscious exposure, it will do whatever it can to keep consciousness out of its life. It will construct an entire life of brass impregnable so that nary a pin of conscious truth can enter. It does this through acquiring knowledge, power or 'experience'.

Conscious truth comes to the self as pain, which emotion refuses to face, anaesthetising the truth of pain with a neurotically safe pseudo-existence. Drugs, obsessive routine, ideological attachments, loveless work, locking oneself away from society and the good old internet are all numbing analgesics.

An analgesic existence creates more suffering—hypochondriacal fear, comedowns from narcotics, the stupidity of addictively clinging to the known and the numb misery of obsessive security—but the emotional self will always choose such suffering over listening to the message of pain and acting on it.

There is no suffering in feeling. Feeling accepts and learns from pain. It listens to the first twinge of pain, of awkwardness, of fear and of 'not-rightness'. It accepts the situation, no matter how much 'I don't like' it and then acts appropriately from there. Feeling is therefore APT and does not lead to regret.

Emotion does not act aptly. It is forever out of step—weird, garish, violent, stupid, forgetful and clumsy. It always does the wrong thing or does the right thing at the wrong time. Acting from emotion always leads, therefore, to REGRET or GUILT. Regret and guilt are the wages of emotion, although they may not always be recognised.

Feeling is apt, or appropriate, because it is empathically one with the situation.[3] There is no delay, no pause, no decision. Such spontaneity is practical and creative, not to mention enormously attractive, but it is a threat to a world built on emotion and, like appropriateness,[4] is punished everywhere in it.

What happens when you act appropriately or spontaneously in the world? I'll tell you, you turn around to check to see if the world saw you. Many, realising this, search their whole lives for a 'safe space' to 'be themselves', outside of the world. They do this because they cannot disregard the world when they are in it. They are cowards.

Ideology and Habit

Emotion is only in love with itself. It only understands itself and it only perceives itself, or perceives the other through the filter of itself. This is why when you are angry, for example, or indulging in self-pity, everyone seems out to get you.[1] Cynicism, along with the many ideologies which justify it, has its roots here.[2]

Ideologies are a means by which emotion can protect and reproduce itself. These ideologies might be atheistic, or theistic, they might be extremely sophisticated and complicated, or they might be a vague kind of 'ordinary common sense'. Emotion is brilliant at choosing just the ideology it needs.

This is why it is so easy for people to change their ideological position. It doesn't seem that way because a single ideology can serve someone for their entire life, but you'll notice when someone jumps from left to right, or from atheism to theism, or from puritanism to hedonism, nothing really changes.

It's also why, as Jonathan Swift noted, it is all but impossible to reason someone out of an ideological position, because such positions are never really founded on reason in the first place, but on emotion (on fear, on desire or on numbed lack of emotion, which amounts to much the same thing). Scratch a philosophy and a heart bleeds.

Emotion doesn't just use Big Ideas to keep itself going, it will grab onto whatever excuse and justification it can get its hands on. It is very good at doing this. No mind is so slow that it doesn't move faster than light to justify itself. It will say, 'I have a *right* to be angry!' or 'it's because of my hormones!' or 'it's all *your* fault!'

Emotion prefers to blame everything and everyone but itself, but one of emotion's cleverest tricks, which it uses as a last-ditch defensive manoeuvre, is to blame an idea of itself.[3] We call this SELF-PITY. 'I am a failure', 'I'll never be any good,' 'I'm just a bad person,' 'I'm weak,' and so on and so forth.

The 'I' in these expressions of self-pity is not the conscious I, but a *conceptual* I, a *thing* that self uses, not as a means of taking responsibility for its selfishness, but of excusing it. With self-pity there is always a sense of hands helplessly thrown in the air, 'what do you expect of a person like me? I just can't help it!'

Emotion doesn't just offer ideologies and excuses, and cling to justifying ideologies, it creates a whole way of life to keep itself going. It uses self to form, as its way of life, a projection of itself in the world. Indeed, it forms, and formed, the world itself. It is no exaggeration to say emotion possesses you, and that it possesses the world.

It does this through HABIT. We are all creatures of habit, which in their place, serve and meaningfully define us, but emotion creates a habit of its whole life in order to protect itself from threatening spontaneity and change. Self does not need to experience raw life when it has the security blanket of habit to hold on to.

This explains why so many people are afraid of new situations and why they refuse to even try to enjoy a new experience or feel something new. Every now and then in your life you'll witness someone who seems to be totally 'together' completely fall apart when faced with the horror of all habitual people, a new feeling.

All this would be fine if habits were confined to the self, but they metastasise into the marrow of the world, a world which must then be formed in their image for the habitual self to function, specifically into the habit-factories we call INSTITUTIONS, which amass, manage and reproduce habits at scale.

Ideology and Habit

This explains why habitual people are so pathetically dependent on institutions and on professionals, and why institutions and professionals destroy spontaneous living truth wherever they appear, imprisoning it, and us, in 'how things are done round here.' We are all victims of the incarcerating effects of highly habitual people.

You have probably noticed this, how restrictive the company of habitual people is, and how dreadfully constraining the atmosphere of institutions and professionals. Again, if in doubt, watch what happens when death appears, or loss, or love, or great beauty, or anything out of the ordinary. Habitual people go out of their minds.

This is why everyone is so profoundly unhappy. I don't just mean that they are in pain or unsatisfied, which are unavoidable. I mean that they are anxious, depressed and angry—emotional. It is, when you think about it, quite amazing that nobody, or almost nobody, in the whole world, is really happy,[4] but there you have it.

Don't try to explain this to people. They'll listen to your words, and agree or disagree, but explanation exists in self, in the realm of opinion, attitude, emotion and belief. And so even if the truth releases geysers of enthusiasm—'yes! yes! OMG, *this* is it!'—you'll find a few months later that it's all dribbled, away, 'oh *that*? Yeah, I've moved on.'

And as we've seen argument won't work. No chance. The mental-emotional self will not listen because it cannot listen. It will find a way round even the most brilliant argument, usually by endeavouring to score points. If it cannot 'win', the self will protect itself by getting angry, and insulting you, or by feeling hurt, and insulting itself.

Only pain works, only pain changes man and woman (especially man), the pain of having your heart-broken— which means having your self broken. There are several ways this can happen, but nothing gets deeper than love. A long, long journey down into the deepest recesses of your being, that begins with the single step of the approach.

Improvisation and Fate

Man moves and woman is moved. Man looks and woman is looked at.[1] Man leads and woman is led. Naturally, there are exceptions, because nature delights in breaking rules and upsetting expectations, thank God, but a man who cannot lead is as unhappy as a woman who insists on being in charge.

Man's authority is primarily in the public or manifest domain. Privately, primarily, he is following *her* heart. Not her emotions, and certainly not her will, but the strange quality of her innermost, which is, like his own, one with the music. If he is dancing to that tune, she will gladly follow him to the edge of doom.

Just as a man who cannot lead is unhappy, so a society, one such as ours, in which men no longer publicly lead (or must do so through force), is also unhappy. The great dance breaks down, and everyone has to do their own thing (or rather, everyone has to do their own thing, and *so* the dance breaks down).

The first step in the dance is for a man to approach a woman. This could be a literal approach, talking to a woman on the bus, for example, or it could be asking a girl out that he already knows, at work or at college. In either case, he approaches her. If he waits for her to approach him, he'll attract unhappy women.

Most men, being repressed cowards, use TACTICS and TECHNIQUES to approach women (chiefly the cowardly tactic of not approaching them at all). He will be nice and polite for example and attempt to wriggle his way into her interest by being a friendly friend. This, to his deep dismay, never works.

Or he will ask hundreds of questions.[2] Or he will manoeuvre himself into being useful. Or he will boast and try and win her with his credentials. Or he'll try to buy her with his fame or his money. Or he will engineer time alone with her and sidle up to her and sort of hope that perhaps she sort of gets the message.

Some women will be taken in by such crude and feeble tactics. Others might be desperate and ignore his clumsiness in exchange for his attention. It might even be possible that, underneath his fearful faffing, she perceives a man of real character. But this is unlikely. Most likely, he's just a child.

Man fails with women because he does not understand that she does not evaluate him mentally, but physically. She senses, in her body, that he is bluffing, that he is concealing his desire for her by being polite (or, if he is particularly immature, trying to conceal his fear of her by being obnoxious).

A woman is essentially a Reichian therapist,[3] able to intuitively detect, through her physical awareness of the tensions in his face and in his body, that a man's psyche is locked up. She can rarely articulate quite what part of his self is imprisoned or why, but her intuitive guesses are often miraculously accurate.[4]

Naturally, I am speaking of a conscious woman here, and women do tend to be more conscious than men; but most women are unconscious, slaves to their emotions and only able to evaluate men in terms of those emotions, which usually comes down to a crude assessment of how much power he has.

That said, she is less attached to her evaluations than he is. Ask her what kind of man she goes for, and although she might offer a horrifying exemplar of caricatured masculinity as an ideal, she is often willing to give up this mad eidolon in the presence of a man with presence. A man who is free and untamed.

This is why extremely ugly men can do so amazingly well with women. She says she wants a square jaw, thick hair, nice hands, wide shoulders and so on,[5] but she'll give it all up in a trice for a man with strength of character, passion for genuine mastery and an empathic awareness of what the hell is going on.

Some men, understanding all this, learn so-called PICK-UP SKILLS, in order to bypass her mind and manipulate her emotions; to compel her, through references to sex, physical contact, ungrasping assertiveness, suggestive body-language and so on, to unplug her brain and continually evaluate him in sexual terms.

By using the tricks of a pick-up artist (PUA),[6] a man (any man) can, with some practice, learn to manipulate woman (*not* any woman), through a combination of raising her emotional temperature, suppressing her critical powers and appealing to her biological weaknesses, into a date and, eventually, into bed.

Not that manipulation is all bad. Up to a point, women like to be 'manipulated'—men too, if the pilot is confident, experienced and skilful. Men who relinquish public control and let interaction with women fall into a vortex of consultation ('I dunno what do *you* fancy?') tend to get dumped, or get saddled with a virago.

At the heart of pick-up scene are (or were, it is now a prudish 'post-game' world) some sensible and laudable principles, above all, to learn to be—indeed, to actively work hard at becoming—confident, attractive to women and capable of handling the excruciating demands of talking to a girl you don't know.

Thus, many pick-up artists really did become 'better versions of themselves', better dressed, better read, healthier, more socially confident, more physically intuitive, more emotionally aware, more comfortable with ambiguity and more sensitive to subtle cues of tone, body language and unspoken implication.

But love, integrity and vitality play no part in technique, which is why women who fell victim to the predatory arts of the pick-up artist so often felt used and exploited, and why men who were attracted to the the scene, including so-called 'masters of the art', were so often small, broken creatures, incapable of love.

Today, the PUA scene has mutated into the 'manosphere', where young men gravitate after being told that they are privileged rapists who haven't dealt with their so-called 'toxicity'. Here they discover they are understood by other men who understand nothing about women beyond warped versions of PUA technique.

Being a technique, woman can learn counter-techniques to defend herself, against the pick-up artist and tiny-hearted 'incel', but she is defenceless, and loves to be defenceless, before a man who hides nothing and who does not use any technique or force to manipulate her; who openly loves her, without predatory sexuality.

Such a man is not ashamed of loving her, from moment one. Today it sounds like the nuclear option to walk up to a lass you don't know and say, 'I love you',[7] but, believe it or not, in the right spirit this can work. Whatever you say though, such conscious pluck is a prerequisite to all interactions with all women.

Real women love consciousness. The weaker ones, and there are many, are swayed by mere confidence, a polished performance, money power or the wafted promise, from a bearded patriarch, of being protected, forever more, in a feathered boudoir.[8] But real women, and there are more than you think, adore consciousness.

But consciousness runs deep. Women, as we have seen, have to respect a man, they have to know that he is living from his own conscious centre and has the guts to live that way no matter what the world tells him is right, or valuable, or handsome, or whatever; and she can smell this from a hundred miles away.

Thus, a man must be consciously loving, but he must also have the rare quality of CONSCIOUS INTEGRITY, commitment to the unfolding of consciousness in time, also known as FATE. Without commitment to fate, he's just another 'non-playing character', wearing a mask that a real woman sees through as easily as if it were a window.

This, again, is why ugly, bald or chubby men who radiate the pzing of essential integrity have outrageously good sex and tremendously fulfilling love lives. Even a total wreck, if he is living from the inside out, as so very few are, has more chance with a real woman than a slick superman with a bolt-on personality.

A man with conscious integrity knows what he is about and doesn't give a tuppeny toss about the consequences, because he knows consciousness will take him where he needs to go. This today is called 'owning it'—taking responsibility for who you are. Is anything more desirable in a man?

Weak men, without integrity, want attractiveness to be about confidence, economic power and physical strength because these are things that weak, loveless men can either *get*, and stay weak and loveless, or blame the world (or women) for not providing. Either way, no need to take responsibility, no need to be a man.

Men with integrity have 'a certain something' that they're willing to sacrifice their lives—or at least their comfort, popularity and niceness—for. Such a man, even if he is a jobless, criminal drop-out, is infinitely more attractive than a stuffed shirt, no matter how many books the stuffing has read or kilos it can bench.

This is why woman is often surprised at who she is responding to, because it's often not the kind of man she *thought* she liked at all.[9] She thought she wanted a handsome man with prospects. Ha! You silly. Heartbreak hotel for you. But in the wreckage of heartbreak you might realise what you really want, what you really, really want.

Conversation and Courtship

First of all then, a woman INVITES a man. He might need to force his foot into the door to give himself a chance, to interrupt her momentum and get her attention. But unless he manipulates her through pick up tricks, he needs her invitation to proceed and he violates her if he goes where he is unwelcome.

Once he has knocked on the door (or twice perhaps, three times at the most... she can respond to a bit of persistence you know) and seen that, through the way she looks at him, through her posture, and through the quality of her voice, that she is giving him a chance, then he may try his hand with a CONVERSATION.

The conversation, if it is to succeed, must be unplanned.[1] It must draw its inspiration not from the past, but from the moment, responding to the situation they are both in and responding to her as she is, in this situation. This is difficult for man, who is less well acquainted with the situation than she is.

But this works for him, or should do. The very difficulty of throwing himself into the void of the moment, unscripted, without a technique, can earn him what he longs for, a slightly impressed smile. Why would he want it to be easy? Only a child needs stabilisers and floats. A man dives in, even though he may drown.

If he persists with her, uninvited, he doesn't stand a chance. If he is grasping and starey, if he sticks tediously to his plans and to his knowledge, or if he tries to win her by force or by bragging, he doesn't stand a chance. And if he is afraid of her, sweating, gulping and stuttering, he doesn't stand a chance.

Probably! For woman, strange creature that she is, and despite what she might say, does not respond to the explicit, literal fact. As we've seen, she hears what he says, but she is listening to what he does not say. If he is clumsy, or violent, or even a complete wreck, he can still possess spirit. He can win her heart by breaking all the rules.

Today we live in a world dominated by literal laws, a 'no means no' society that demands explicit consent at every stage of courtship, right up to orgasm. This makes it impossible for man to prove his mettle, which is to say, his judgement. He no longer knows when to break the rules, when to be audacious.

There are some advantages to such a world; every form that a nightmare takes allows for a reflected version of waking. Today, women are better protected from the violent force that male-led societies allow, if for no other reason than that men now lack the energy to kick down her door. But at what cost?

Woman responds to audacity, but he must know the right time for it. It's not what you know, but when you know it. Woman expects man to know *when* he should ignore everything she is saying and abseil into her bedroom, and *when* the game is up.[2] He should, in short, be able to read her heart as well as the room it is in, *now*.

Man tends to lack either sensitivity or courage. Some men are quiveringly aware of what is going on in women but lack the balls to do anything about it. Others are swashbuckling heroes (or think themselves to be) but haven't the foggiest what's going on in her bellymind. We call the former COWARDS and the latter BASTARDS.

The bastard, usually found in the upper and lower end of the social scale, must learn to perceive the aura of phenomena, the quality of things, the vibe of the room. He must learn to quieten his will, so that the strange voice of unself can speak to him. Then his audacity will have a purpose nobler than gratification.

Conversation and Courtship

The coward, whose home is the middle class, must learn to act despite how he feels. For courage is not feeling no fear at all—which is psychopathy—but acting despite it. Thus, even though man sweats and stutters and flaps around, his character, manifest through his courage, may still charm her.[3]

Approaching a woman requires courage because it is a form of IMPROVISED THEATRE, which demands total exposure. What this means is that something more profound than the mind, the emotions, the will or the appetites of the body must be in charge of the situation. This 'something' is consciousness.

The unconscious self cannot bear to talk to another person, particularly a stranger, without relying on tactics, props and scripts. These include gagging, gassing, gossiping, questioning, flattering, judging, grandstanding and controlling, either through violence or through titillating excitement.

If, as noted, the unconscious self has sufficient power or prestige, through fame, money, or through its position in society, it has no need to rely on any of these tactics, which is, for many men, the chief appeal of success and money-power, and why these things tends to be synonymous with mediocrity and charlatanism.

IMPRO demands innocence. You cannot create something from nothing if you go in with the something of your personality, your beliefs, your knowledge and your appetites. You have to open yourself up completely to the moment, or you'll get trapped in the abominable clench of 'this is not working'.

You'll notice this if you plan what to say to her. You'll also notice it if you reuse a witticism or charming comment that seemed to work well elsewhere. You'll also notice that it is extremely difficult to talk to her if you don't do so in the precise moment you have the chance, and instead let desire build up.

The safe and easy way is to meticulously plan, come in with a load of impressive facts, engineer romantic coincidences, or rely on your money, your name, your prestige, your influence or the power of your parents. To throw yourself into the improvised unknown without such props demands great courage.

Being approached *by* a man also requires courage, albeit of a different kind. A woman has to let her consciousness run free, so to speak, and share her sweet nature with the world. She has to be consciously available for love, available to be admired and enjoyed, and surprised, by men of all ages.

Such availability necessarily allows jackals through the door, which is why women walk through the world with nary a glance to the left nor to the right. A sensible approach for undiscerning young women, but those who can tell the difference between a grasping and a giving look need no such defence.

She *must* open her heart—or it will expire in her breast—but she must also have faith in its power to discern prince from predator and pretender. This is difficult because her emotions are fearful (attracted to the kind of security which bores her spirit) and weak (attracted to the kind of excitement which breaks her heart).

The solution is to discover unconditional love, the source of love in one's bare life, before it is clothed with the conditional pleasures of attention, affection and security, which all depart. This is a life's work, and beyond the limits of this enquiry. Nevertheless, you can start here, in this little room.

If you cannot feel love unconditionally in your body, here and now, before you meet a man or woman you will, first of all, by the same miraculous attractive principle that draws bastards to cowards and exploiters to the easily exploited, you'll bring to yourself a love that rests upon extremely shaky, and very conditional, foundations.

This principle, a kind of 'relationship karma,' governs all love with a merciless, punishing—and ultimately glorious—logic. And although it demands an improvised, open-hearted and gendered spirit, it has nothing to do with what you know, what you can do (e.g. your 'game') or what you have, but who you are.

To put this another way, if you have anger in you, someone is coming to make you angry. If you have jealousy in you, someone is coming to make you jealous. If you have fear in you, someone is coming to make you afraid. And if you have love in you, someone is coming to love and be loved by you.

The second consequence of living without unconditional love is attachment. Without a love that does not go away you'll cling to the 'love' that does. You'll tell yourself that your love is *there*, in him or her, and not *here* in your consciousness. As clinging is repellent at the cellular level you'll then drive the object of your love away from you.[4]

Unconditional love is the surest defence against deception. How can you be deceived into buying something you already own? Another defence, for woman (who has a lot more to lose from poor judgement), is to refuse to have casual sex with a man, particularly one who is pestering her to sleep with him.[5]

A man must prove himself, first of all with his conversation. Can he really listen to what she is saying? Is he bold enough to cut through her prattle, and sensitive enough to say something real to her, something she loves to hear? Or will he moan and whine to her, or fill her with questions, or talk to her as if she is another man?

A man must also prove himself with time and with patience. He must be able to demonstrate that he loves her enough, and loves life enough, to be able to wait before making love with her. He must woo her. Otherwise, chances are, all his charm, humour, considerateness and patience will evaporate after an orgasm or two.

Or after encountering her diabolic emotion, which will mock him, set traps for him, blow hot and cold, incite his jealousy, needle his impatience or lash out for no good reason. A man must face something of this nature, sooner or later, in his woman, and he must face it *like* a man, with the unemotional power of presence.

Woman has a tendency to think man is a simple creature, that he only wants one thing, because that is true; but it is not the truth. The truth, as difficult to locate in an ordinary man as a bat in a cave, is that what he wants, more than anything else in the world, is to realise his true nature and to love woman through that nature.

As we have seen though, this is not just a state he can access, but a fate he must live. He must, through his life and work, realise the truth of his spirit in the world. Not a simple task, so profoundly complex in fact, and lonely, and difficult,[6] that woman has as much chance of understanding it as he does of understanding pregnancy.

If a man has not discovered what manliness is, or thrown himself into uncertainty, or been broken in solitude, or touched the wild within—none of which woman can teach him (indeed mummy will do what she can to thwart him)—he will grow up to be just another fearful, institutionalised sponge-cake, hated by woman.

Does this mean that woman must wait for a Prince of Love to come along on a white charger? If so, she'll be waiting for more lifetimes than the one she has. No, she 'only' needs a man who is on the way to a better place. As he isn't there yet, she must expect all his tediously predictable fears, desires, tricks and tactics.

Fortunately, she has a defence against man's self. Not a defence she is conscious of, for consciously she is at his mercy. It is not her mind that protects her from loveless man, that stops his satanic self from getting into the Garden of Eden, but something far deeper and more disturbing. The FIENDESS.

The Fiendess

The tests that a woman puts in the path of a man are both conscious and unconscious. Conscious, firstly, in that she *knows* he must prove he can master his desperately desiring self before she'll let him in, and secondly in that she *knows* she must be courageous enough to cast him out forever if he cannot.

Her unconscious challenges to his self-control are more terrible. As the prince gets closer to her heart, he finds it circled around with a forest of thorny emotions. Erratic bursts of spite, fickle wilfulness, chilling indifference and even hatred come at him. Hard. She knows, by instinct, just where his weak spots are.

I am speaking here of the fiendess, the diabolic emotional self implanted in woman by man's world. If, as Barry Long says, 'he cannot walk away' from that self, and detach from the emotions of rage, fear and self-pity that it seeks to arouse in him, it will crush him, an event he is not likely to forget.

If all this seems rather unfair, it is because the man in question knows himself, and his world, but slenderly. He cannot see the supreme truth of heartbreak, nor can he see that the problems he has with women and the problems he has with the world are one and the same. This is why he can rarely handle either.

With each trial man must consciously master his self; his cowardly fear that he will lose her forever (he might you know!) and his bastard desire to control her through force; through physical force or, more likely in the modern world, through force of technique, force of capital, force of argument and force of desperate effort.

Few today understand the difference between FORCE and POWER. Force is a *wilful*, mechanical effort to change an external situation. Power is conscious energy, or *willing* surrender to still, present, consciousness. Force is blind, unconscious energy. It is restless and clumsy. Force creates problems, power solves them.

Men do not understand the difference between force and power, and excuse their force—which always depends on external strength (the strength of muscle, money or management)—as power. Women do the same, and are often attracted to force, stupidly thinking that they will find power behind it.

You can see the consequences of this confusion everywhere. Men everywhere running around trying to acquire external force so that they can get what they want, and women either falling over themselves to get at the most forceful man in the room, or giving up in disgust at the whole sorry show.

Man must therefore overcome his urge to force the situation, and woman must overcome her urge to submit to force, excuse it, or fight it with force of her own. If he is unable to do this, to separate from himself, he will remain a child, and seek to acquire muscle, money or management to make up for his deficiency.

To put all this another way, every step of the dance demands improvised self-abandonment, and not just in the approach. At every moment with a woman, man must sacrifice his mental-emotional self to the presence from which he gathers the spirit either to hug her, despite her tyrannous emotions, or to walk away.

It is usually the bastard who must learn to hold on to her thorny heart and the coward who must learn to let go of it. But in either case, man must find courage to face emotional demands that he must painfully walk away from, love to face cold spite that he must painfully embrace, and discernment to tell one from the other.

For a man to be worthy of a woman takes many years of such trials, well beyond courtship and deep into the far lands of marriage. But it is at the start, while dating, that a woman must discover if the knight has the gumption to make it all the way to the dragon's cave. Unless she does this, she will have her heart broken. Again.

As for him, he'll get nowhere without heartbreak, which is to say, without SELFBREAK. If he ever rises to the challenge of love (unlikely in a world comprising men who are only ever vaguely conscious on a Sunday afternoon[1]) he will be, sooner or later, torn open by it. Then a new, better man may emerge.

Have you, man, ever met a woman who totally ruined you? Who you gave everything to, and she took that everything and crushed it to pieces? No? Well, that's why there's not much to you. Or perhaps you have, and all you learnt from the lesson was how to be more careful, how to avoid the risk of sacrifice?

What about you woman, have you ever met a man who loved you with everything he's got, and it wasn't enough, so you broke his heart, or made his life a living hell, perhaps despite yourself? Have you ever destroyed a man's false self, not with hatred, but with love, so that a finer soul might emerge from the rubble?

Probably not, which is one reason love is in such a dreadful state. Men do not give enough of their hearts to go through heartbreak and women pander to men so that they'll have to accept what little their shrivelled up hearts can give. a little bit of excitement, a little bit of security, a little bit of pleasure. A little bit. Not much.

This is why your relationships are so insipid or full of bitterness and contention. This is why you roll your eyes and tut and switch off when your partner is speaking. This is why you are so unfulfilled, intellectually, emotionally and sexually. This is why your orgasms are rare, brief or shallow. This is why you are fucked.

Sex with your Self

Self seeks relief from the misery of emotion in distraction and stupefaction; in work and wealth-gathering; in gossip (including the news); in righteous indignation and worry; in mindless chatter about the past; in food; in drugs; in mindless fun (sport, travel, pointless hobbies, and spectacular entertainment); but above all in SEX.

Indeed, all distractions are really just a stand-in for sex, which is why so many of them have a vaguely sexual nature, why gossip is often salacious, why warfare, sport and chasing the dollar provide a kind of erotic payoff and why food and other sensual pleasures (even the design of technological gadgets) are regularly described as 'sexy'.

This is why young and highly excitable men are plagued with premature ejaculation, because they spend their lives in a state of sexualised agitation. When the moment comes to actually enter a woman they're so worked up, they ejaculate. For a few moments they are aware of the shame of this, before they set off again…

Unless the self has been numbed by the world, it is frantic to seek sexualised narcotic distraction and stupefaction through emotionally exciting sex. This does not provide self with the freedom from emotion it yearns for, only temporary satisfaction. Emotion, which is to say, suffering (discontent, boredom, misery, etc.), soon returns.

If the self is able to have as much sex as it wants, because it is extremely beautiful, famous, powerful or rich, it ends up being destroyed. You can see for yourself how ugly such selves are by looking at the fucked-up faces of sexual has-beens, upon which all the emotion of the desperate sexual wannabe has manifested.

You can also see for yourself how quickly emotional 'love'—the selfish experience that the loveless world calls love—turns to hate or indifference. You may have noticed in your own life how the big love of your life, the person you wanted above all others, turned out to be an object of hatred or indifference.

This doesn't just play out over the course of the relationship, but even over the course of a single day. Everything is sweet and dandy, and then, from out of nowhere, a wave of emotion hits you both and you are suddenly separated by a gulf wider than the Atlantic. It is at that point you experience for yourself SOLIPSISM.

Solipsism is the theory that only the self exists. Very few people seriously believe this,[1] but everyone experiences solipsism for themselves. When you are possessed by emotion, you might know other people exist, but they appear to you on the screen of a mind that is radically SEPARATED[2] from the other.

To consciously experience the solipsism of self is horrifying. Indeed, to realise you are trapped, here, in this self, eternally separated from the inwardness of the other, from the situation, from reality itself, is to not just realise that you are in hell, but that you are all the devils that comprise it.

It is good to realise this though (particularly for man, who is innately more solipsistic than woman), for how can you free yourself from a prison you don't know exists? Only through the horrific realisation that it does. This is why a man who hasn't seen he is in a hell of his own making is almost certain to drag you down into it.

You glimpse the horror of solipsism in the flat, dead eyes of other emotional selves, or in the jagged feeling you have in their company, and you fall into the nightmare of it if you have sex with them, the feeling from which is like two people masturbating over the idea of the other, because that is what is actually happening.

That is why the feeling of orgasm after masturbation feels so similar to a loveless sexual orgasm. Sex can occasionally lead to furiously intense orgasms, but in any case, the self, directed towards a point of release, the orgasm, is merely being satisfied. There is no real joy, because joy is not a point, a *thing* that can be achieved.

Both masturbatory and sexual orgasms occur at the peak of expectation and pleasure, coincident with ejaculation. With a loving orgasm, the height of pleasure and emission are not related; in fact, orgasm and ejaculation may not happen at all, or, if they do, they may hardly be noticed.

The wages of sex is pain. Loveless sex always leads to suffering. Always. Sex will crucify you; on the cross of your own miserable self, which becomes, with each loveless, self-informed orgasm, more and more thing-like, more and more caricatured (i.e. like itself), and, as we shall see, more and more alienated from eternity.

This is why the pleasure you get from masturbation and sex can be rated, but to give a score to making love would be as monstrous as to defend its value.[3] The pleasure of lovemaking is not QUANTITATIVE, it is QUALITATIVE, and as such, only metaphor (which is to say, only art and myth) can express it.

In lovemaking, a woman has a series of cascading orgasms, or, just as likely, no orgasm at all, but the whole experience is orgasmic. He may or may not come, but if he does it will be rather a delicate affair, a snowflake orgasm, followed by an extremely intense culminating plateau of pleasure.

After lovemaking he feels awake, still aroused, because the orgasm is not exciting, not an 'up', which means there is no [come] down. Sensation is absolutely direct, without being filtered through relative expectation. There is no need of 'release' because there was no tension that accumulated beforehand to let go of.

Sex with your Self

In sex, if she's very lucky, she has one or two orgasms, possibly intense, but *brittle*. More often than not, she doesn't come at all, and feels short-changed. His orgasm, at the very peak of the event, tapers off immediately into a sleepy withdrawal, from which he gradually recovers in a distant, irritable mood.

This irritable feeling, once the sleepy aftermath of orgasm has passed, that one is not closer to the other but further away, is due to sexual solipsism. It afflicts both sexes, but it is harsher in man, which is why woman becomes fearful, needy or pre-emptively cruel after loveless sex; she knows pain is coming.

Chances are though, the pain was already there. For many women sex is a deeply unsatisfying encounter with an emotionally stunted adolescent mind. Most are familiar with the essential loneliness of sex, of wondering what on earth they are doing there. Another woman would serve him just as well.

To put all this another way, the male orgasm, like the male penis and the male self, is MANIFEST; it exists in the represented world of the self. The female orgasm, like her vagina and her essential being, is UNMANIFEST; it touches the source of consciousness, before it appears as any kind of thing, action, idea or feeling.

This is why woman, to man, is such a mystery, why, to make love with her, is to enter a inside-out reality which only myth can express—the myth of death, entry into the underworld and rebirth—and why to protect himself from the underworld, he remains in his self and he fucks an image of her self.

When man has loveless sex, or masturbates, he has an orgasm unconnected to anything else in the universe, whereas when he makes love with a woman, his manifest orgasm, or ejaculation, which her manifest body experiences, is followed by her unmanifest orgasm, which his consciousness experiences.

This is why, first of all, loveless sex and masturbation are just so pitifully, sordidly *sad*, because there is an inherent solipsistic loneliness to the experience, and why they tend to lead to guilt (particularly in the man), the recognition that you have done something wrong, which is to say, selfish and unloving.

And it is why the more powerful the loving orgasm, the less intense the male ejaculation feels, until it very often doesn't happen at all. The whole experience becomes her orgasm-in-itself, which his manifest self is unfathomably one with. Again, only art and myth can present such a state without it sounding bizarre or cheesy.

To summarise, lovemaking has nothing to hide; sex is ashamed (or shameless). Lovemaking intensifies awareness (colours are more vivid, music sounds lovelier); sex sends you to sleep. Lovemaking is delightful, joyous, and laughably, exhilaratingly strange; sex is a hard, serious, comprehensible business.

I say 'business' because solipsistic sex is a kind of work, and like work it demands technique. I do not experience the other from the inside, and so I must find ways to understand and manipulate him or her. First of all, to get the other into bed, then to get myself (or, if I am a 'generous lover' both of us) to orgasm.

The bedrock of sexual technique is fantasy; pornographic imagination (of someone else, someone not in bed with you), elaborate role-play, narcotic stimulation, ridiculous costumes ('cosplay'), sex toys and all the other accoutrements of kink. As we've seen, self needs such props in order to get sufficiently excited to enjoy itself.

And, as mentioned previously, as self ages these gimmicks become more and more necessary, particularly for the insensate male, leading to the desperate perversions and dependencies of 'dirty old men' who can't get themselves off without stimulating imagery, extravagant role plays, ghastly perversions or popping blueys.

This isn't to say that props and techniques are necessarily wrong, but that the solipsistic self relies on them and in its reliance becomes numbed to the direct experience of making love, which leads it to being hooked on more and more exaggerated, extravagant and perverse games (and surrogates for lovemaking).

In fact, when it comes to sex, technique and kink are unnecessary. Love is everyone's kink. You don't really need to know or do anything special to make love; you just need to love and the body will do the rest.[4] The simplicity of this is horrifying to the sexual self, which is why it scornfully refers to it as 'vanilla'.

Likewise, you don't really need to learn anything to find or win a partner. Learning has its place, and understanding provides power, but the essence of approaching a woman, or in being approached by a man, is deeper than anywhere knowledge can reach, because your whole life is involved.

And so it is with making-love, which is why guides to making love, like any other 'self-help', are, by themselves, next to useless. You can solve problems by 'solving problems', but you can only solve *the* problem by solving, or *dissolving*, your entire self; by dying, entering the underworld and being reborn.

What this means is that, to be in love with another, you have to both be capable of letting go of yourselves, of existing together in absolute, selfless stillness. Unless you can both share nothingness together, enjoying each other at the deepest, darkest possible level, all the surface light you share will cause you pain.

Nothingness is a most unpleasant, unsettling and downright freaky place for the ever-moving, ever-thinking, ever-emoting self. It seems boring to thought, and it feels cold to emotion, and horribly strange to both. And yet only here, where self meets unself, can you ever really be together.

Male and Female Sexuality

Let us remind ourselves, before we go on, of the essential difference between man and woman. Man, as we have seen, and as many primal folk recognise, is born incomplete and must discover his wholeness through his fate. Woman, as messed up as she is, is yet whole and need only uncover what is already there.

Man, to put this another way, is *disembodied* until he has fought his way back—with manly courage—to the wholeness that woman was born with. This is why he is more insensitive than her, and why he makes a better killer, a better butcher and a better scientist,[1] because he can more completely detach from the sensate reality of life.

It is also why man is a more abstract, propositional thinker than woman, and why their conversation so often breaks down, as he, valuing well-defined definitions, continually asks, 'What do you *mean*? Is that *true*?' while she, valuing evocative impressions, continually responds with, 'What do you *feel*? Is that *good*?'

And it is why disembodied man is sexually obsessed. He is a split, selfish creature, frantically 'in love' with his propositional idea of her. She learns the nightmare of this demonic, bodiless sexuality sooner or later, but in her innocence she can barely imagine the depths of his sexual desperation and the violence of his pornographic desire.

Most men, despite their blather, are sexually repressed, which leads to a division between their day and night selves that is as comic as it is tragic. Woman is familiar with the experience of being charmed and excited by a confident, in-control man's man who, as soon as she takes her clothes off, transforms into a cretinous maniac.

Some men have powerful wills, which can stay in control of a powerful libido in extremely arousing situations. Other men have suppressed or drained libidos. The beast brings hollow sexual pleasure to a woman, the gentleman, no sexual pleasure at all. Not really much of a choice, is it?

Man represses his sexuality, pretending by day not to be a sexual creature, in order to stay in control of his affairs, and to please, reassure or seduce women who are afraid of male desire, or disgusted by it. He keeps the beast zipped up in his gentleman suit, although it takes a sneaky look out of his eyes when it can.

Then, when the opportunity arises, if the curtain of social convention is lifted, and particularly if he has worked himself up, through imagination, or through adrenaline, the beast emerges, in all its true horror. If you're in any doubt about this take a look at how soldiers tend to behave with women during wartime.[2]

A man who is not repressed is a rare creature. Such a man has discovered something that can control his demonic energy far more effectively than the suppressive will. This PRESENCE, unlike will, does not suppress sexuality, but transforms it into love. He is a sexual animal by day *and* by night, but such sexuality is not bestial.

Woman's sexuality, despite strenuous assertions to the contrary, is but a shadow of man's. The most unhappy and restless of women, enmaled by the world, become deformed into the sexually voracious VIRAGO or man-made NYMPHOMANIAC, but to live with such poor creatures is, until they have been tamed, hell on earth.

The intensity of woman's sensuous *love* however, and her need and desire to be physically loved, makes man look like a cock with its chicken cut off. This is why, although her neuroses can be so easily played, she has so much more power over her sexuality than he does, and why she needs such a long build up to sex.

Life, Play and Passion

Making love evaporates the pain of sex. Anxiety, neediness, desperation, indifference, attachment, sentimentality, frigidity, anger, tyrannous emotionality, fear of commitment and the universal tragedy of solipsistic loneliness; all dissipate with love making. All that remains is unconditional love.

Unconditional, being necessarily selfless, is not made with selves. There is therefore, ultimately, no emotion in lovemaking, nor any rational self-awareness, because the love that is made 'precedes' emotionality and rationality. It cannot be grasped with thought or desire. It is mysterious, which is why it is proper to call it SACRED.

The word 'sacred', like its near synonyms 'divine' and 'spiritual', is entirely without meaning in the modern world. It was stripped of the mystery it refers to first by religion and then by science. This is one reason why it is so difficult to talk of matters of importance, such as love and lovemaking.

Drained of the sacred, lovemaking becomes solipsistic fucking, with as much mystery to it as scratching an itch. Modern herbivores rarely have enough spirit to leave the house, let alone find someone to have sex with, but when they do stir from their solitude, they usually find a shared coffee provides more intimacy.

And so making love begins with a sense of the sacred. If this does not exist in the house, there is no hope for love. Sacredness is not RELIGION, which, like atheism, is a means to insulate man from spiritual truth. Sacredness is a the living, sensuous mystery, manifest in myth and meaningful metaphor, that pervades qualitative LIFE.

Life, Play and Passion

By *qualitative* life I do not mean the abstract, *quantitative* idol that the sacrilegious world worships.[1] This spiritless 'thing life' is not experienced in the body, it is an abstract statistical object that is measured, manipulated and managed so that the body, and beyond that existence itself, can be controlled.

Nor, by life, do I mean mere LIVING, or worldly existence, which comes and goes. Life does not come and go. It is always here, and so it doesn't need to *get* things to be content. It is not weighed down with fear of *not* getting, nor does it need hope to make it through the day. It is not a *thing* that has been left behind or is on its way.

Making love, therefore, starts with life, and a shared, selfless sense of its quality—its sacred goodness—from morning to night. In that goodness there is ease between you, humour, happiness, interest, tenderness. It may not be all fireworks and delight, and there may be grievous difficulties, but life is here, and it is always here.

To put this another way, if you cannot love unconditional life (again, not conditional life/living; *nobody* can love that!), you cannot love another person, for the simple and tragic reason that your attention is directed on an external form, which will leave you, as all things do, putting fear and desire between you and it.

If you put your attention, *first of all*, on the other, you cut yourself off from them. It is not, first of all, love for him or her that brings you together, because he or she is a form, or partial expression, of life. It is only love for life that unites you, that takes you out of your self and into the other, into the whole, that you share.

Your love, in other words, must have a purpose. Not a goal, something you are trying to get, but a sense of something finer than your own desires. You could call that purpose 'God', but even putting aside the degraded connotations of that word, it's odd to talk of 'sharing God'. Sharing life makes more sense.

Sharing life, all day, is real foreplay; love play. You may well enjoy what the world calls foreplay—'sexual activity which precedes intercourse'—but this is not really necessary to make love. If there is love of life between you all day, you can make love at any time; if there is not, lovemaking is next to impossible.

Unconditional love, therefore, cannot be switched on and off. It must be lived, or felt in the body, throughout the day. This is not an *'of course I love you'* love,[2] a love that you 'know' you have for someone, but an actual sensation of love, in your body, which reaches out to the other from morning to night.

If this love is not present, it is impossible to make love. The whole day is foreplay, because the whole day is for PLAY, not for mere FUN, the narcotic pressure valve demanded (and manufactured) by the unfun working world. No, *play*; loving largeness of spirit that releases focused attention from the anxieties and desires of self.

For love is not just passively *there* in your self, any more than life is, or health. It must be actively, playfully, made, or realised, which means you must give love, give loving attention, and act to reduce the emotionality (excitement, fear, desire, indifference, pride) that gets in the way of that gentle attention.

Giving loving attention to your lover doesn't therefore mean giving presents (although it might) or 'consideration' (although it must). It doesn't mean doing, thinking or saying anything in particular. It means giving yourself over to the other, just as you must do with everything and everyone else in life. This is PASSION.

Passion means giving up your partial self, and all the bits it focuses on, for the *whole* life of the moment, in this case, a moment filled with your lover's presence. Where a passionless, sexual lover is into partial ideas and sensations, a passionate lover is into the complete experience; the smell, sound, appearance and feel of the other.

Because passion can only ever be of the whole, it diminishes all partial problems. Where the passionless man or woman focuses on the partial problem (the pain, the fear, the worry), thus amplifying it, the passionate man or woman experiences a whole present which contains, and thereby diminishes, partial negativity.

Presence also diminishes constant, low-level, sexual WANTING, the curse of the walking-talking penis that ejaculates as soon as a woman opens her legs and the reason why it plunges so readily into substitutes for the vagina; above all, as we've seen, sport, business, violence, and lust for power.

The passionate man has no great need for an objective thing, projected into an abstract future, to feel happy, for the whole can only be experienced here and now. He has desires and ambitions, but they do not reduce the moment to an objective bridge by which these can be reached.[3] The moment is sufficient unto itself.

Reducing the whole of the other to an objective thing is the 'OBJECTIFICATION' that feminists who are no longer young enough to be subject to 'the male gaze' complain of, but which woman actively colludes in by taking advantage of man's thirst for things, by *enjoying* his objectifying attention and by submitting to his objectifying world.

Active passion therefore means the ability to separate, or pull back, from the hyper-focused self. This is no easy matter, and requires a lifetime of practice. In order to experience the whole of the other, your lover, you must be able to experience the whole of the street, the garden, the beach, the train, the room...

Active passion also means ACKNOWLEDGEMENT, of *recognising* the present whole, in this case the present whole of your lover. You acknowledge the lovely way he looks at you or the way she feeds the cat so sweetly, or the good influence she has on others or his mighty integrity, or whatever it is that brings you happiness.

And if nothing is bringing you mighty joy, if there is nothing you can acknowledge in him or her, then something is horribly wrong, and that wrongness will come back to you as the horrible condition of your existence. Because, the just but dreadful truth is; you get what you acknowledge.

The more you acknowledge the good in your life, the health you enjoy, the interesting work, the comfortable bed, or whatever good there is in the moment, the more good will come to you. More love. If you acknowledge, as most people do, the problems, the worry, the fear and the misery, you'll get more of that. More emotion.

Sometimes emotion seems almost impossible to get rid of. If you've indulged yourself in reckless worry or morbid self-pity, if you've over-excited yourself with porn, violence or salacious gossip, or if you've spent eight hours straight in front of the dead screen, you may have built up too much emotion to love.

By being selfish in this way, by thinking and by being true to the wanty-wanty feelings that result from thinking, you build up so much emotion that it can take hours, sometimes a day or two, to flush it out. The solution is not to indulge your self at all, but if you have done so, you need to fairly burn with passion to reach beyond it.

Sit down with each other and talk of love, of death, of each other, of the moment. Work up a furnace of love or, even more powerfully, say nothing at all and be still together, gazing into each other's eyes. That might be enough to break through the solipsistic wall. It might be wonderfully easy. Or it might take some tears.

Only this way, by breaking through the castle wall of the self-informed self, can you unite the whole kingdom. Only this way, by allowing your still consciousness to reach into your lover, can you keep the strange oneness between you alive. Only this way, by being in love all day, and acknowledging it, can you make love every day.

Courage and Sensitivity

This is all well and good, you women might be thinking, but how do I reach my man with love? He is so proud; take even one itty-bitty step towards his fears and desires—his anxieties and addictions—and he explodes. Just a hint of a criticism and he starts to simmer or darken. He's just so damned stubborn! He *will* not change!

He loves you, yes, we know that—but does he love you enough? If not, leave him. Break his heart. It's the only way he'll learn. Do you think love will change him? No chance. It would change you; of course it would, you're a woman. But love won't change a selfish man. As we have seen, only pain works with men who cannot love.

But then, if you leave him, that will mean being on your own, perhaps forever. The horror! You can't do that, can you? You can't give up everything you've put into this relationship? And what about the children!? No, no, you'll just have to keep your head down and make do as best as you can, and hope things will one day get better.

Such fear and such hope (hope being fear's public relations department) keep the whole loveless world turning. You have to be braver for love if love is what you want from life. This is why love demands profound courage, or FAITH. Not faith in an idea of life (or of 'God'), but faith that life will actually look after you if you act for love.

And if you don't really want love, if other things are more important to you, such as security, safety, ambition, comfort and fun, then you have no reason to complain. Live your loveless, faithless life like everyone else, clinging to a loveless situation, in the vain hope that it will magically change, as your life dribbles away.

But you might be one of the lucky ones. You might be a woman with a man who will listen. Some rare specimens do listen to woman—to her, not to her emotions—and do what it takes to be worthy of her love. Such a man can be told to raise his game, to do better, and, slowly, he can grow to be worthy of you.

The rare ability to listen is one of the two qualities man must have to be worthy of woman. It's very unlikely she'll find a real man from the off, one who has mastered himself and realised his fate, but she can find a man who has what it takes to get there; COURAGE, which is a kind of passion, and SENSITIVITY, which is a kind of listening.

A man might be a clumsy lover, a crude thinker or an emotional cripple, but if he can listen—first of all to the situation and then to the people in it—he is capable of overcoming all these problems and more, because he is capable of overcoming the self-informed self that separates him from his own consciousness.

Capable, I say, but whether he does or not is a question of courage, the passionate will to overcome the little voice of self which tells him to stick to the safe and secure path, the known. He may intuit the truth, but does he have the balls to act on it? If he does not, he cannot be trusted. No matter how nice a coward is, he'll let you down.

Courage, in fact, is so valuable, it is respected even when every other virtue is absent. This is why men, particularly young men, are so keen to display it. The problem is that man usually lacks the sensitivity required to know *when* to be courageous, which makes him merely reckless, like a child.

Women do not have this kind of courage. Her courage is to do what she knows is *right*, which is why he admires her, not what is *true*, which is why he finds it hard to trust her. She is mortally afraid of revealing her truth to the world, which she sacrifices her identity to so that we all might live in peace together on this hateful rock.

Courage and Sensitivity

For the truth she needs a man. His courage is to act when he does *not* know what is right or wrong, and to trust that whatever the consequences are, he'll have the gumption to handle them. This maddens her, but she loves and admires it and cannot live with a man without such pluck because she needs the true like he needs the good.

Really though, although it is useful to separate sensitivity from courage, the two are one. You cannot really listen unless you have the courage to overcome your self and all its opinions, and you cannot really act courageously unless you possess the passion that comes from listening to—and really hearing—the truth.

This is why when woman is dating a man, she must pay close attention to how courageous he is and what kind of courage he has. How does this man face authority, how does he cope with failure, how does he deal with his phobias? Is he courageous enough not just to take care of your soul when the going gets tough, but to realise his own?

And woman must attend to how sensitive he is, how carefully he listens to the situation, and to you. Not necessarily to your words, which might be awkward blether or risk-allergic social-pandering, and certainly not to your emotions; but to your heart. Does he hear your silence, or does he just react to what you are saying?[1]

If man cannot listen or if he is not courageous, he is not really a man and should be avoided. Leave him to his pornography, his business and his games. And if you've wound up in a relationship with such a man, there's little you can do. Words will get nowhere with him. As we've seen, only pain will reach him, the pain of heartbreak.

It is woman's task to break man's heart, over and over and over again, until he is sensitive enough to reach into that within him which is deeper than the heart, his consciousness, and courageous enough to do something about it. When he does that, when he overcomes his stupid ego, you'll be happy with him.

Man on the Moon

But what about her? You men (and perhaps one or two women) reading this might be thinking that I am glorifying woman, putting her on an unreachable pedestal? It's easy to love her when she's the angelic beauty you fell in love with, but what do you do when she transforms into a demonic termagant and flays you alive?

If you are looking for consistency in a woman you are living in the wrong universe, but there are two kinds of inconsistency. One is of feeling, which is, to man, an open invitation into the quality of the moment that it is fused with. The other is of emotion, which is a private—and, for the most part, monthly—affair.

Once a month the two of you will have to face the intense spiritual challenge of MENSTRUATION. It is not 'spiritual' in an airy-fairy sense of requiring religious practice or a new-age identity to face, but because it demands a depth of consciousness that only a word like SPIRIT, for all its clichéd overtones, can evoke.

What happens during menstruation is that a woman's psyche radically alters as she discharges, along with her menses, the suffering of living in a loveless, alien, man-made world. Emotion then swells in her, and she becomes, at best, a dark presence on this good earth, at worst, a right fucking handful!

The deep CHARACTER of woman that man loves so much becomes overwhelmed with her PERSONALITY, the surface form of her self. This is why menstrual unhappiness manifests differently in different women, although it's not *that* different—it's always moody, unhappy and emotional.

Men get the worst of it of course, particularly the closest man to her, because he represents man's world. He will feel her disdain, he will be aware that she is treating him like a bumbling child or like a hopeless fool, or that there is an unpleasant sense of duplicity about her affection, like she's forcing it.

Some women become obsessively fussy during their period, sometimes with material matters, sometimes psychological ones, treating those around them as dirty objects. Some become needy and whiny, some savagely critical and some unbearably scatty. Some retreat into an awful brooding darkness, others become hollow and distracted.

And that's if he's lucky. If she's having a bad month, or a bad life, then, once a month, she'll turn into a veritable gorgon. As Barry Long once said, *'it's hard to believe that she could exist outside of hell'*. Unreasonable isn't the word. What on earth did you do to deserve all this rancour? You're innocent here aren't you?

Nope. You have to take responsibility, man. Certainly, she is the one holding onto her suffering, not you, and finally, only she can let it go, so if she cannot, or will not, you might have to leave her to it. Yes, she is responsible, but if you don't take responsibility for her pain (or recognise that she is defenceless before it) you're doomed.

I'll explain, although it might sound weird. All the irrational pain that is flying into your face is not hers, it's *yours*, reflected back at you from her heart. You are getting from her, what you give, or what you have given, to her and to life. This is why her period is always worse when you've been neglecting her.

Think of it this way: It's your period too. You have to face it as your own diabolical creation. You have to stand up both to her emotions and to yours, and refuse to bend to them, which means, first off, refusing to argue with her and refusing to get into all the whys and hows that emotion throws up, in its search for an argument.

Emotion wants an argument, because that produces more emotion. You have to detach from that, not coldly, with aloof disdain, but with affection. You must not speak from all the emotion (i.e. irritation, anger and pride) that the situation will stir up from you. If you do you'll say something that sets off more emotion.

It's difficult because objectively she *is* wrong. Yes, yes, you're quite right; she really *is* being unreasonable. To argue seems like an easy win. It would be with a man, you could crush him; but this is not a man you are dealing with. She is radically different from you, and your normal, rational tactics simply will not work here.

Rationality starts with appearance. With the fact that your mind presents to you. What she is saying and doing, when she is at her worst, is factually false, but (assuming we are speaking here of a sane woman) *morally* truthful, a moral truth which you must face morally, which is to say, with love.

Even the base fact of her material appearance is false at this time. During the pre-menstrual period she looks uglier. Puffy, lank, pale, blotchy; as emotion fills her heart her face becomes heavy and grim. This then warps your perception, and you *see* her as ugly, even when she's just as pretty as she was a few days ago.

This isn't just the case with older women; even the hottest, youngest, 'ten out of ten' goddesses look awful when pre-menstrual emotion warps your perception of them. It's quite interesting really, from an objective standpoint, how this lovely creature can suddenly look so weird, wrong, like a gargoyle, a witch or a monkey.

But of course there is no 'objective standpoint' when you're in the thick of it. Jesus Christ, it's coming at you from all directions. It's like kayaking down a river of blood. All the while your mind is telling you, with absolute factual accuracy, that you are right here—and yet here you are drowning!

Sometimes she is so good at hiding the hard, dark little nut that her soul has become—from herself as well as from her man—that he is at a loss to work out why he feels bleak, frustrated, tense, on edge. It's strange. There doesn't seem to be any reason at all, although his mind comes up with all kinds of possibilities.

If he then voices one of these possibilities, or acts on one of them, he'll get in hot water. She will find it *extremely* difficult to say, 'It's not me'. She will at once cling to her emotion, justifying it, while, if he dares to point it out—'Oh, I see, your period is coming'—lash out at him for trivialising her feelings.

What all this means it that man and woman must, once again, take responsibility for their emotions, and not blame them on each other, on the world, on bad luck, on 'chemicals' or on anything else. It's not her fault you feel the way you do, and it's not his fault, it's *my* responsibility and *our* task to realise that.

Notice that the world does everything it can to prevent men and women taking responsibility for their pain. Where DEMOCRACY, which allows everyone to blame everyone else for their ills, is the chief vector for *social* irresponsibility, PSYCHOTHERAPY is used to prevent *individuals* from taking responsibility for their lives.

The world doesn't want you to realise that *you* are the reason you suffer, because if you do, you'll stop handing over your responsibility—which is to say your power and freedom—to professionals. No, you must be convinced that your vices are not vices at all, but MENTAL ILLNESSES, fuzzy theoretical objects that you need *treatment* for.

Nothing much has changed in this regard for centuries. Where once your difficulties with your wife or husband were caused by the devil, today they are due to rejection sensitivity dysphoria, dependent personality disorder, hyper-sensitivity, ADHD, PTSD, issues of abandonment, past trauma and so on and so forth.

Once, you would have had to go to a priest to get your mind right. Today you must go to a therapist. In both cases your *own* perception and understanding of the situation, and the sensitivity, intuition and power required to face and deal with it, are devalued and disparaged, and sometimes actively punished.

Don't stand for it! *You* must face your emotional possession. *You* must release your attachment to substitutes for love. *You* must stand up to whatever or whoever is feeding your emotions or playing on your attachments. *You* must take responsibility for your mediocrity, your insensitivity and your inability to love.

You, nobody else. Of course, sometimes you need to talk, and of course, sometimes you need help. And, as the old song has it, woman needs man, and man must have his maid. The point is, one more time, if you are unhappy in love, the responsibility lies, ultimately with *you*. Not with your parents, your partner, or the world.

As Barry Long taught, you are unhappy because you think and because you are true to your emotions. You are *not* unhappy because of the situation. Everyone blames the situation for their problems. But the reason you feel the way you do is because you will not, in the moment, give up your anger, fear, craving, indifference or pride.

You might not be sharp enough to do this, and then the black iron cage will descend, and the two of you will be split at heart. The house will become a stifling prison which you both yearn to get away from. Emotion will infect the children and corrupt everything you do, together or apart. Then, finally, a storm will hit.

If there is enough love between you, the storm will be a squall, if not, it will be a tornado, but whatever happens, if you face it rightly, the wall that divides you will fall and you will find yourselves in a happy land again. If you make love, it will be joyful. You'll wonder what on earth happened. Until next time.[1]

Making Love

What all this means is that to really be in love, you need to build up a certain amount of conscious power, which means you have to stop frittering it away in unconscious DISTRACTIONS[1]; fidgeting, over-eating, gossiping, wanking, worrying, useless fantasy and scattering your conscious attention over the hyper-distracting screen.

If you cannot do this, a constant, low-level hum of emotion will buzz away in the background of your awareness, making you unsettled, anxious and restless. Thus distracted, you'll find it impossible to handle any situation which requires presence and power; presence to feel out the truth of what is happening, and power to address it.

Such situations include living in wild nature, talking without a script, being alone without devices, approaching a woman, creating something meaningful or beautiful, dealing with humans directly (without the protective buffer of power), facing death, being a beginner and dealing with anything that is really new.

You'll notice that the world makes it very easy to avoid these things. The more worldly you are—which is to say the more easily you can, through technology, wealth, institutional authority, or the influence of fame, force situations to submit to your will—the less real you are, or ever have to be.

Indeed, it is no exaggeration to say that the world was created so that man could avoid reality, so that he would not have to live in the heart of nature, act spontaneously, be radically alone, deal with his fellows directly, confront death, face a new life-demand, approach a real woman, or make love with her.

No experience on earth is as real and immediate as making love. No experience *demands* as much power and presence, and no experience *gives* as much, which is how you can tell that almost nobody has really made love, because so few desire the power or presence to make it, nor have the gravitas and lightness of spirit it confers.

You can also tell that almost nobody has made love because nobody speaks as if they have. They never talk about what it actually feels like to make love, because they don't know. All the depictions of lovemaking in all the films and novels of the world speak more for what their directors and authors don't know than for what they do.[2]

And if people don't speak like they've ever made love, they certainly don't look or act like it. Men and women would not carry on as they do—compromising with the vicious demands of the world, working without real purpose, living in constant fear—if they had made love and felt the reality of it in their guts.

Not that you need to make love to experience love. The truth of love exists in the body of the earth before it manifests in the body of a lover, which is how those who are close to that earth, or who have never made love— young children, for example—can be so loving, so free and so sensitive to strange frequencies.

But even if love begins in the simple, solitary human heart, no human heart will ever be closer to you than that of your lover. It is only there you can discover what the body of the earth really is. Only in your lover's innermost can you overcome the horror of the sexual world and reach into the flesh of eternity.

So why doesn't this happen more often? Once again, it's his fault. Faced with a woman's body, the majority of men are like an orangutan trying to play the violin.[3] Some men learn sexual technique, and can bring their partners off one way or another, but very few can really touch a woman, really smell her, really feel her.

And once again, this is not to say that women are innocent. As we have seen, countless women today are disembodied, lacking in sensuality, and strangers to passion. But it is up to man to remedy this. Not through mere skill, but through physical presence. Not through getting off on what is happening, but through adoring it.

Adoration is another word that has lost its potency. It now sounds vaguely ridiculous. Worship too. No man or woman today would take seriously the suggestion that you should *worship* your lover. But this is precisely why the unimaginable pleasure of conscious lovemaking, the kind that Krishna and Radha once made,[4] is beyond them.

The pleasure from lovemaking is so great, so intense, that it's hard not to believe that you won't pass out, or die. It is a shattering experience, and yet, at the same time, nothing much appears to be happening because nothing much is happening to the sexual self; to the mind and to the emotions.

Thus, when you are in love, and in bed together, everything will happen naturally and easily, but only if you can keep the mental-emotional self in the background. This means that the emotions—particularly sexual excitement, anticipation and anxiety—and the mind—with all its imagination and chatter—must be silenced.

If emotions are involved you're unlikely even to get into bed, particularly if you're in a long-term relationship. You'll listen to your feelings, which will tell you that you 'don't feel like it'. Making love has nothing to do with such selfish feelings, or lack thereof. Making love happens whether you feel like it or not.

If emotions are involved, a perspex layer of self will come between you, upon which the self will paint alluring pornographic images. He'll probably enter the cinema of his self before she does (if he ever left), but, unwilling to be left outside on her own, she'll soon follow, leaving two separate selves getting off on themselves; masturbating.

Emotional separation manifests as thought, which nearly always means that something is wrong. It's the same with any other activity. If you're watching a film and thinking of something else, the film is no good. If you are playing a game and thinking of something else, the game is boring (or you are playing it badly).

Thus separated, by emotion and thought, everything seems to be wrong. She shouts in your ear, he pushes too hard, there's a funny smell, the neighbours are talking in the next room, that didn't feel right, I really must clean the fridge. The mind doesn't just respond to such distractions; it all but magics them into being.

To overcome self in bed is therefore the same as doing so at any other point in your life (which is why it is so hard in bed if you *don't* do it in the rest of your life). You have to passionately give your self over to the whole moment, you have to acknowledge the good and spill yourself into it, into all of your senses.

To soften your attention into the whole moment, means pulling back from the concentrated part. This part might be the desire to fuck or be fucked. It might be anxiety about your performance. It might be the stupid irrelevant thoughts you are having. Or it might be a restless tension in your chest or a pain in your head.

Whatever it is, the solution, or *dis*solution, is to widen your awareness. You must kiss without tongues, you must keep the light on, you must talk to each other, you must look in each other's eyes, you must let your attention spread to your whole body, your neck, your nose, your legs, your ears...

Speaking during sex helps. Speech takes the self out of the isolated imagery of the event and into the shared temporal flow of it. Speech can be turned to diabolic excitement and absurd fuck talk, but it is a natural movement of the spirit, which delights to hear love and gendered-surrender poured into its ears.

If one of you gets lost in the self, the other must bring him or her back. You must stay conscious together, utterly conscious. To the old masturbatory way of fucking this might seem at first rather peculiar, even clinical; this is because sex is a kind of drug, and going cold turkey feels empty at first.

You must confront any emotion as it arises. It may be there before you get into bed, which means you have spent the day lovelessly, not sufficiently present together. Or it might rise up as you get closer together. Loving honesty is the only way through this barrier, but, as we've seen, it may not break without a storm.

You must move extremely slowly. This is important as he enters her. When he is inside her, there is no need to move at all. Loving stillness will open her up, deeper and deeper. He will be amazed at her depth and how much power there is in it. As this power breaks over you both, you may think, 'I can't believe it!'

Such unbelievable presence softens the concentrating self and enables it to act more naturally in bed, without self-informed sexual desire or self-informed sexual anxiety[5] coming between you. With your attention softened, something else is in charge, something bigger than the both of you. Far bigger.

Slower and slower, stiller and stiller, more and more loving, the separate self passes away. Go deeper and die. There are still two bodies, now more vividly incarnated than they have ever been, but the sense of self that separates them has gone, leaving the oneness of love that everyone yearns for.

A literal description of such an extraordinary experience inevitably sounds fantastic, clichéd or 'spiritual' to the ordinary mind for the same reason that all literal descriptions of conscious truth do, because they transcend the coordinates of the literal mind. In truth, making love is so simple and ordinary that the literal mind misses it.

And this simplicity might even include a touch of kink or of filth. When there is enough love between you, of the whole, a degree of partial sexuality—not to mention a *great* deal of raucous sensuality—can find its place without getting out of hand and sending you back into the self that gets off on it.[6]

So we can say the *definable* side of sex may or may not be filthy, may or may not involve wild sensuality, may or may not be fast, silly or savage; but the *indefinable* side, which must come first, is and always is present, tender, loving, slow, incarnate to the tips of the fingers and impossible to speak of.

Definably, or literally, two bodies *fornicate*, indefinably they fuse in the *fornix*, the underground cave of the self, which is only acceptable to ordinary men and women as myth; as passage into the cavern of sleep, as battle with the dragon of the self and as reawakening, or rebirth, into the wholeness of being both dreamer and dream.

What *can* be literally said is that the loving orgasm is simply amazing. Every time it happens, you just cannot believe it. Laughter is common. A couple who do not regularly break into splendid laughter upon orgasm—a long, long orgasm—is like a forest that doesn't burst into birdsong when the sun comes up. Such a place is dead.

It may take some time to get back to life. Most people have years of accumulated emotion layered over their psyches. Their genitals are numbed, tense, unconscious; *private* parts. They are without the passion, and therefore without the intense presence and spontaneous character, to reach the other, or to be reached.

There will be frustration and failure. But that's alright. You love each other, don't you? Love is patient. So this time it didn't work. Let's walk barefoot in the garden for a bit, or read poetry to each other, or make a radio show, or have a shower together, or cook something elaborate. We'll make love again soon.

Submission and Domination

Woman, as Barry Long wrote, has been brainwashed into believing that she must give to man, that her pleasure comes from being a sexual servant, or from taking the active role. The truth is the reverse of this; the most profound sexual experience man or woman can have is when he gives to her. And gives. And gives.[1]

Giving means giving up the thinking, wanting self. This is the passion of man's love, total absorption in her physical existence. Not hard, creepy, objectifying concentration, but passionate en-joy-ment of her presence. This will turn off her brain and silence her emotions, and create the reckless pleasure in her that man loves so much.

Such giving does not mean fawning over her, asking for her consent or labouring away to give her an orgasm. That this is all the attention egoic man knows how to give woman is the reason she turns away from lovemaking, becomes jaded or, in edgy frustration, takes on the role that he cannot, of active loving.

Likewise, being passive (in the sense I am using this word) does not mean that she gives up her power to spontaneously act in lovemaking (which is one of its greatest delights for him), or to lie like a wet towel while he works away at her. It means she gives up her emotional need to get somewhere. This is divine humility, or ABASEMENT.

Abasement (again, as I am using the word here) means HUMILITY; to lower one's pride before the other. DEBASEMENT means HUMILIATION; to lower one's integrity or intrinsic worth. A woman who cannot abase herself will never be happy with a man, and a woman who needs to be *de*based will never be happy with a man either.

Naturally, we are speaking of a man that woman can trust, who loves her, and who has spiritual authority, that is, power over his self, passionate consciousness of the present moment and enough character to face the world, including her worldly emotions. Without this, she cannot and will not give herself up to him.

A degree of abasement, of surrendered humility before his spiritual power (assuming he has it), is natural in a woman, a touch of sluttiness if you like. When this gets out of bounds, it becomes an unnatural desire to be (or perhaps an indifferent acceptance of being) degraded, used, choked, hurt and fucked.

A degree of assertion is also natural in woman. Woman has a simplicity, directness and 'erotic courage' that is appealing, and that man longs to appeal to, or to please. When this gets out of bounds it becomes a demanding hunger to be appeased. In extreme cases, as she ages, she becomes voracious, not for love, but for relief.

A weak caricature of man, an exaggerated personality with no intrinsic authority, must force woman to submit, and a weak caricature of woman, who needs to give up her will, must submit to him. Male and female cyphers then object to such male violence and female complicity, and condemn male domination and female submission.

But characterless cyphers are just as constrained, just as violent, as egoic caricatures, the only difference being that their instincts to dominate and submit are displaced onto the institutions they serve. They can no more give up their bland, ungendered morality than caricatures can their garish hyper-gendered appetites.

A strong and confident woman who freely consents to follow[2] her man's lead is no more subjugated than a man who freely consents to submit to her strange authority. Both cyphers and caricatures fear, and therefore hate, such freedom, which is why they fear and hate abasement and reverence.[3]

To put all this another way, caricatures cannot escape status and must engage in grimly serious rituals of humiliation, while cyphers obliterate status entirely and cannot engage in gendered status play. Neither know love, the zero-status which makes subordination and domination an enjoyable game.

Evacuated of reverence, domination becomes a diabolic desire to humiliate, and submission to be humiliated. Anal sex and the standard money-shot of porn, ejaculating on a woman's face, are examples of the lovelessness of a man incapable of reverence and of a woman content to pander to his selfish desires.

Contemporary culture makes a sin of domination and submission themselves instead of their desacralised and profane reflection in the sado-masochistic ego. By doing so, by outlawing divinely joyful domination and submission, sexuality itself is deracinated, which of course is the point of the perverse world.

Thus uprooted, sexuality becomes either a plasticky parody of itself, as the monstrous violence and grotesque degradation of porn amply demonstrates, or it is hollowed out completely, leaving little more than casual, spiritless, unfeeling transactions ('booty-calls', 'friends with benefits', etc.) between spiritless nothings.

The solution, the end of all this fucking horror, and the fucking horrible world it creates and sustains, is to find someone to love, to court her, or be courted by him, and then to make love, each and every day. This is the realisation, in the world, of all the love stories we never tire of listening to.

But the love stories we read always end when the prince kisses the princess. This, fighting dragons and dispelling evil charms, is a truthful reflection of the psychological reality of romantic love, but it does not reflect the material reality, which doesn't end with the kiss, but begins with it.

After the Honeymoon

When two people first come together in love, it's all kinds of wonderful. There's sweetness and delight, marvelling sex, romantic days out, delightful discoveries... You tell your friends, you make plans, 'Everything's going to be like *that*... and like *this*...' But that doesn't last very long. Suffering is on its way.

After the honeymoon, normality lands like a sack of rubble, bringing a cloud of compromise with it. The romance fades and a battle of wills begins, a long wearying campaign, punctuated with pleasant truces, but finishing in defeat for both sides, and much bloodshed. For most people, that's just how 'love' is.

The problems usually begin about three months after moving in together. It's only when you've made some kind of commitment, and can drop the 'date face' that you maintained to win and woo him or her, that the old painself, the unhappy persona your parents taught you to adopt, emerges.

Then we see the hurt, mopey child. Then we see the foot-stamping and the tantrums. Then we see the hot outbursts and the cold sulks. Then we see all the old tricks that baby used to get attention, or that the little boy used to shield himself from emotional hurt. Then we hear the lies, the whining, the begging, or the cruel barbs.

Strange how wrong you were about him! He seemed so nice, funny, capable. She seemed so sweet, giving, attentive. You thought you'd hitched your life to a grown-up. But something has changed. The self you fell in love with is not the one you're living with. Someone, or something, else has taken its place.[1]

After the Honeymoon

You wonder what to do. Actually, you might think, this mysterious goddess is really rather boring and ordinary. Or spoilt. Or clingy. Or cold. Or erratic. All the intriguing mystery has gone. And isn't he weak? Cruel? Selfish? Rather an imbecile really. You shouldn't be expected to live with this! It's not fair!

One of you now wants to get away from the relationship, and the other wants to hang on to it. But there was no great commitment to begin with, to keep you both together, and so it is easy and all-too common to act on your feelings and part. Usually it is he who breaks her heart, but the roles could be reversed.

People don't stay together for long today. The pill, the washing machine and the 'career'[2] have 'liberated' woman from the need for long-term relationships, and a world which forces her out of her body has taken away the heart she so loves to give to a man. So she hops from one lover to another, with a minimum of fuss.

And he is even more ready to move on. The world, being the supreme expression of the male ego, serves his wilful fear of commitment at the expense not just of long-term fidelity, but of even trivial, symbolic expressions of duty, responsibility and obligation, such as making a move or paying for a meal.[3]

This is why it is so easy to split up, to drift between casual relationships. The modern world is arranged so that men and women never really have to face themselves, or to face each other. This isn't really her idea, although she takes what advantage from it she can. It serves him, or it appears to.

Nevertheless, people still have long-term relationships. But although they may use the word 'love' to describe how they feel about each other, and although love occasionally makes an accidental appearance, it is not love—real love—that keeps them together. Indeed, they can hardly be said to be together at all.

The Bond of Fear

It is not love that keeps people together, but FEAR. Fear of being left alone, fear of pain (the pain of heartbreak), fear of upsetting one's cosy habits, fear of ruining the lives of one's children, fear of losing one's mortgage or one's business and fear of the opinions of others; parents, priests, neighbours or friends.

Love plays very little part at all. The word 'love' might occasionally be used to describe how people feel about their partners, but on closer inspection this 'love' turns out to mean a mixture of habit, affection, dependency, loyalty, attachment and, if they are lucky, like-minded friendliness—all fine, to be sure, but not love.

Love, as we have seen, is something which actually exists, in your actual body, now. If you don't actually feel love, the lovely warm flowing sensation of it,[1] connecting you to your lover, then your love is, ultimately, mental or emotional. You can look inside and find *something*, but that something is not love.

It's like an anxious, angry or numbed person saying, 'I am conscious'. If you are emotional you can no more be conscious, than you can be spontaneous, creative or light-hearted, because emotion has suffocated the source of consciousness, or of spontaneity, or of creativity, or of light-heartedness. Or of love.

Indeed, without real love the affection, dependency, loyalty, attachment and like-minded friendliness that people call love also wither and crumble, because they were rooted in a shared truth which has dried up, leaving the outward shell of it. This shell might seem friendly and stable, but it is anything but.

Think of your parents. Think of other long-term relationships you know of. If you cannot perceive miserable, suffocating coupledom, characterised by bitter compromise, deepening, deadening misery, frosty indifference and emotional cruelty, then, most likely, you cannot perceive the relationship at all.

Some long-termers are very strange indeed. Some couples don't speak to each other at all, except to discuss daily practicalities. Some sleep in separate rooms and never make love. Some know nothing of each other's thoughts, know nothing of each other's fears and desires, know nothing of each other at all.

And it gets worse. Couples, as we have seen, appear nice and stable and loving, because it is so important for them both to do so, but, at night, she turns her face to the wall, he sighs for women he can never possess. This dread misery leaks out in icy little put-downs that couples publicly prick each other with.

None of this is difficult to spot if you're conscious (softly aware that is, not slyly scrutinising). The lack of physical flow between man and woman, the underfeeling of separation, the sour glances they shoot at each other, the tension in the jaw, the tightness in the lips... all of these outward signs are the tip of a miserable, loveless iceberg.

Sometimes, in the worst of cases, couples make no attempt to conceal their profound indifference towards, or even hatred for, each other. Then we can be sure that their home life is a living nightmare of emotional or physical suffering. These are the relationships that we ordinarily call 'abusive'.

But all relationships that are not founded on real, day-to-day, minute-to-minute love, in the flesh, are abusive, because the unconscious, unloving self that conducts them is *inherently* abusive. It may be brilliant at concealing this squalor—big smile for the neighbours—but it can't cover the nasty smell.

Caricatures and Cyphers

Actually though, there are two basic species of relationship weirdness. The first is found between degendered CYPHERS, in whom passion has died. Here we find a seething pit of frustration and hatred in such pairings, but it is suppressed, pushed under the surface, from whence it periodically erupts in ugly outbursts.

This bloodless cypher-coupling is more commonly found in the modern, professional-class, FRATERNAL West (which includes the wealthy, Westernised professional class in the East). Alienated from the gendered reality of the body by the technolotrous system their discarnate minds manage, they become hollowed out, gone inside.

The misery of the cyphered relationship is often hard to detect, because the middle-class are so adept at PUTTING ON THE FACE. A significant body of great narrative art is devoted to exposing or parodying the gulf that separates the clean, 'adjusted' professional-class facade from the rot that it conceals.[1]

(Great art, that is. The substandard mythoi of the cypher is devoted to justifying the blank, loveless, degendered nothingness at the heart of the institutionalised management-class relationship, which appears in television and literature, over and over again, as entirely normal, albeit wistfully tragic.[2])

Perhaps you happen to know, from the inside, a *lovely* middle-class couple, in a 'stable, long-term relationship', a programmer perhaps, and his wife who is a doctor, or two graphic designers, or a successful businessman and his wife who 'writes'? Lift up the lovely, stable lid of these pairings and worms crawl out.

The other kind of basic relationship pathology, more common in pre-modern, lower-class and non-Western PATRIARCHAL societies, can be found in long-term relationships between hypermale and hyperfemale CARICATURES, in which ritualised abuse has taken the place of the natural status play of healthy masculinity and femininity.

The caricatured male-female pairing is the *historical* norm, in that it emerged with civilisation and formed the ideological basis of history, conceived by patriarchal man as a non-stop war against woman and all that she represents—empathic sensitivity, sweet innocence, wild nature and unconditional love.

As we have seen, the myths of civilised man reflect the petty ego of the caricatured hypermale, who values weakness in woman (weakness that is, not softness), who seeks to justify and excuse his violent domination of woman (and nature) by blaming her—woman the deceiver, the seductress—for his fears and desires.

Today, the doormat wife, who chooses emotionally reassuring debasement over love, paired with a brutally insensitive apeman, is a classic exemplar of the caricatured long-term couple, still common all over the world, including here in the West, although it has, over the past century, given way to its cyphered opposame.

The shadow of caricatured patriarchy, is, as we have seen, cyphered fraternity, the rebellion of jealous sons against the father's power, which is brought down and replaced with a new totem of 'equality', an idolised image of 'nature' that replaces gendered relations with an artificial mother, or *alma mater*.

Today in the hyper-fraternal West, one is more likely to find, in the caricatured *and* in the cyphered couple, an unnatural child-man living with a virago. He, without the courage, confidence and excellence to handle her emotions (or without the violence he once used in place of such manly authority), gives in to them, 'for a quiet life'.

Her power over his self (including her mothering, which his numbed, baby-self also gives in to) superficially gratifies her emotions, while leaving her sexually frustrated and spiritually unfulfilled, a void she fills with escape fantasies, shopping and manic-obsessive hyper-interest in her children, which stand in for his absent love.

Thus, the caricatured self is as alienated as the cyphered self, but not through an excess of mentation, but of emotion; the pathological fears and desires which motivate the lower classes and which, without the power of detached deferment that the management class learns, deform gender into a parody of itself.[3]

And so, tidy, tasteful, fraternalistic couples torture each other in a different manner to untidy, tasteless paternalistic couples, and each looks down on the other as repulsively prissy, fragile and cold, on the one hand, or as repulsively crude, insensitive and violent on the other... but the loveless nightmare remains exactly the same.

The same torment, everywhere. The same daily wearing away on each other's exposed fascia. All couples know, by ingrained instinct, the precise sore spot, the raw nerve that recoils when touched. Or they just ignore each other, and let the love within them wither and sink into a hard, grim, suffocating everydayness.

And nobody cares! The misery of the loveless home, despite being the cause of all the world's problems, never registers as a cause for real concern. Nobody ever really talks about it. Certainly, people complain about their miserable love lives, but nobody seriously recognises or addresses the horror of lovelessness on earth.

Think of all the outrage there is in the world about war, think of all the op-eds and blog articles written about man's horrific treatment of nature, think of all the books written about the nightmare of history. Then compare that with how much attention is placed on the omnipresent, never-ending nightmare of love.

Feminists *appear* to have taken up the banner, but it is not raised against lack of love, but against objectification, abuse, toxicity, abuse of power, pay grades, glass ceilings and various second-order effects of lovelessness. Feminists do not use the word 'love' because they don't know what it means.

Or rather, they *only* know what it means. Maybe you only know what love means too, like you only know that water is clear and wet, that it contains two hydrogen atoms and one oxygen atom, and that you need it to live? That's fine; the question is, are you drinking it? Because if not, you'll die.

Caricatures die by violence and cyphers by indifference, but as relationships age, they all tend to get smothered by familiarity, a layer of radioactive dust that kills what it settles on, dividing dying flesh from dying flesh. The lips kiss, but there is nothing there, just matter. It might as well be someone else's body.

The source of familiarity, of taking the other for granted is, again, lack of actual love and, as we have seen, it's usually his fault. He gets bored and starts to find his work and his private interests more important than actively loving her, and she then starts to become a normal, ordinary woman in a normal, ordinary world.

A man who has stopped winning a woman—which means stopped giving her loving attention—settles down into the base state that she then finds tedious, predictable and ridiculous. He loses his mystery because he has stopped loving her mystery. An affair is just round the corner, or a breakup.

Without love, over time, the psyche, like the body, hardens and coarsens, which makes the excitement of sex more and more difficult and the comfort of familiarity more and more appealing. Eventually, only spirit can bring you both together, which means, without spirit, you are forever alone.

Fitting and Suiting

Love is felt through the things of the world. Everything is, by dint of its brute existence, lovable, which we sense as the non-hierarchical WHOLENESS of life, but things also express life in more and more conscious forms, which we recognise as the hierarchical DIFFERENTIATION of life; some things are [a lot] more loveable than others.

To put this another way, we live in a universe of *both* EQUALITY *and* of INEQUALITY. The lowliest bumble-bee has as much value and beauty and worth as the grandest emperor; while, at the same time, we love irises more than stones, frogs more than butterflies, dogs more than mice and human beings more than any of them.

At the same time. By itself, the [largely right-wing] hierarchical view of life is monstrous, and leads to a hellish Darwinian war of all against all; but by itself, so is the [largely left-wing] non-hierarchical view, which leads to the suppression of excellence and hyper-tolerance of criminal perversity. Both must be true.

Thus, anyone who cannot love all things, as a whole, and see consciousness everywhere, is broken in some way, defective, and doomed to a sadistic need to control or a masochistic need to be controlled; but so is someone who cannot see grades of consciousness, and so loves animals more than humans, or plants more than animals.

Thus, the most conscious thing in your experience, your partner, is simultaneously the most lovable thing in the entire universe and, at the same time, as lovable as a breath of dust floating across an empty room. If you cannot feel the former, you won't be attached enough; if you cannot feel the latter, you'll be far too attached.

Thus, without a deep, impersonal foundation, rooted in an unconditional acceptance of the whole of life, love becomes frustrating and contentious; 'Who's wearing the trousers here?' But without a wide, personal attachment, love becomes hollow and passionless; 'I dunno, where do you want to sit?'

To put all this less abstractly, long-term love for another is founded (and in its absence founders) on the power and capacity of two people to passionately share the still, dark depth of life, which we can call FITTING, and, *at the same time*, to dispassionately share the bright, moving width of life, or SUITING.

Two people who fit have an intensity of union, rooted in the flesh, but passing beyond it, into the unfathomable. Sex between those who fit is intense; communication, magical. Those who suit, understand each other in the world and can live together in harmony, sharing their tastes and opinions without conflict.[1]

What tends to happen is that men and women find themselves fitting someone they are deeply attracted to but cannot live with, or suiting someone they can live with but are not deeply attracted to. In the first case there is BOREDOM (having nothing to do); in the second, ENNUI (having nothing to be).

You may have noticed, reading books from times past, how amazingly quickly men and women seem to fall in love and get engaged. There is a courtship period, but it's an odd, compressed affair. This is because, prior to modernism, most people (or most people of the same class) suited each other tolerably well.

Or you might have witnessed for yourself how often, in some cultures, arranged marriages seem to work surprisingly well. It shouldn't be possible, given the unique needs of the human heart, for one's parents to be able to find a wife or husband with whom one can live with for decades, and yet often it is.

Again, this is because distortions of individuality in the hypermodern West do not exist in other, pre-modern, parts of the world. This is not to justify arranged marriages but to point out that it is easier for rural peasants in Kerala or Jakarta to find someone they are suited to than it is for university students in Brighton or California.

In the modern world life has fragmented down every possible fault-line, which makes finding someone with the same outlook and taste maddeningly difficult. An arduous search is necessary to find a partner with whom one can watch films, listen to music and discuss politics without falling into separation.

But if finding someone who suits you is hard, finding someone with whom you fit is, in a world comprising shallower and shallower selves, becoming next to impossible. This is why modern relationships, rooted in the casual, glancing touch of a trivial heart, have as much chance of surviving as a tree planted in sand.

Fitting is, as we have seen, a matter of 'modal' compatibility. A female mind seeks a male mind, a male body seeks a female body, a female will seeks a male will, a male heart seeks a female heart, and all the innumerable gendered divisions and subdivisions within these aspects of self have similar polarities which seek their opposite.

Suiting, on the other hand, is not so limited by modal compatibility. It is not opposites that suit each other, but similarities. The mind rejoices in its reflection, in that which understands without having to be told. This is one reason why people who are perceived to look, think or want the same as me are given preferential treatment.

There is therefore, and will always be a certain tension between fitting and suiting, because what suits the daytime self turns out to be very different to what fits the underworld of attraction that gendered polarities produce. People often find themselves madly attracted to people whom they would otherwise detest.

Fitting and Suiting

You must fit, and you must suit, but it goes without saying that it is neither necessary nor desirable to seek a 'perfect' union. Part of the fine pleasure and the noble purpose of being together is to deepen each other towards better fitting and widen each other towards more harmonious suiting; to change each other.[2]

That said, if you don't have moments of telepathy, if you can't share each other's pleasures,[3] if you can't make superb love, if you do not laugh at the same things, and if there is not an electric current flowing between you, you are either heading towards a breakup, or towards a pit of humid, unloving long-term coupledom.

The question is, if it's not right now, will it ever be? Or if it is right, will it continue to be? How do you know if you fit and suit? How do you know he's Mr. Eternity? How do you know she's the one? Simple. *You* don't know! You can *never* know. It is known *for* you. If *you* get out of the way, it is clear that he or she is someone to be with.

There is a sense of choicelessness in such unions. As Marcel Proust wrote, *'it is a mistake to speak of a bad choice in love, since, as soon as a choice exists, it can only be bad.'* If you choose your partner, you'll regret it. If your parents or your society chooses, you'll regret it. Harmony comes from absence of choice.

You wait and wait and wait, and then *suddenly* she is there. *Suddenly* he is there. If you are sensitive to life, you'll know it even before he or she is *fully* there. The back of her head, the way he walked into the room, even a signature, even hearing someone's *name* is enough to awaken the quiet sense of rightness that love brings with it.

Then, there you are together. All is easeful. The sun shines brightly, shopkeepers are unusually friendly, help comes from nowhere. Problems come, horrible ones, but you get through because you want to get through. You have no choice. Something bigger than both of you is at work here. It is time to get married.

A Ritual of Commitment

Marriage is no longer common in the West, for much the same reason that formality, small talk, courtship, dressing for the public, thanking God for one's food, taking Mass and celebrating coming-of-age are out of fashion or heading that way; because ritual has died. Rationalism has no need of it.

Marriage, in truth, is a ritualistic gesture of commitment. It carries meaning, as all rituals do, through an irrational performance of affirmation, of participation in the irrational quality of the moment. In the case of marriage, we affirm our commitment to live together and to share 'the moment' for as long as possible.

Not forever (although, as we shall see, love is forever). Nor even for our whole lives, for marriages can end. But for as long as there is love between us, and for as long as there is the will to make more love. For all that time, stretching as far as we can see, we are committed to participating in 'the moment'—in life—together.

Marriage, like all acts of love, is an act of service, from the man to the woman. It is he who must give up his independent need to ejaculate into every vagina on earth, and it is marriage that ritualistically affirms this. This is why wives tend to feel more secure in their love than girlfriends.

Men fear commitment because they fear giving up what they believe makes them men; the power to do as they please. They look upon the stamped-down cuck that marriage has made of weak men, they look upon all the women they will have to give up (at least in their dreams) and they think; no thanks!

This is why bastards do everything they can to keep a relationship on a casual footing, to keep their options open for as long as possible (even while married), and why cowards run into the arms of a nice, secure, dependable long-term partner who will take care of their unused testicles.

Marriage, insofar as it represents man's complete surrender to the soul of woman (which, of course, is possible without the ritual), is, for he who is able to rise to the almighty challenge of it, an ordeal by fire that rewards man with the finest expression of his masculinity, a sense of wholeness which only long experience can provide.[1]

This is why those who have faced and mastered the dragon of self—as it manifests in the punishing emotions of woman—have a *gravitas* that homosexuals, celibates and casual lovers (who never take on the dragon) and cowards, cucks and nice-guys (who are defeated by it) do not have.[2]

It is also why, as we've discussed, the words 'wife' and 'husband' *feel* different to 'girlfriend' and 'boyfriend'. They feel deeper. Naturally, such a feeling is opaque to modern-minded rationalists who see in marriage, as they see in all rituals, little more than an embarrassing, almost childish, expression of outmoded conformity.

Not that the ritual of marriage cannot be, like all rituals, perverted and corrupted, in this case by turning the living sacrament into a manipulable *thing*—a document—secured not by life itself, but by a mere professional—a religious professional (a priest) or a secular professional (a lawyer).

Getting the marriage into writing serves fearful, unconscious, unloving men and women,[3] who, unable to tie the other to them with the sovereign bonds of love, must use external, worldly authority to do so. Wherever the law (religious or secular) binds men and women, you can be sure that love lives not in that place.

A Brief History of Marriage

Marriage, being an irrational commitment, does not, ultimately, conform to any rational calculus. It may well lead to the stability of society and to the moral health of children, but it is, ultimately, a *personal* (yet shared) leap of faith, resistant to reason and to the reasonable, constructed order of society.

This is why tyrannous authority has, throughout history, gone to such strenuous lengths to govern and manage marital relations. In pre-civilised societies arranged marriages existed and were often coercive, but they were still a human affair, sacralised socially by the tribe, and dissolved by the individual man or woman.

The fall of man into civilised time and space saw the fall of marriage into a stultifying network of social taboos designed to tie men and women to the reproduction of social norms. Founding society on property put a premium on the legitimacy of heirs, and therefore on virginity, guaranteed by marriage.[1]

Where no property was involved,[2] these concerns faded. Among the poor, marriage was less about guaranteeing lineage and more about securing survival, weakening man's obsession with virginity. Civilised morality serves economic interests rather than innate virtue and so, without inheritance at stake, sexual norms relaxed.

Civilised societies demanded obsessive patriarchal control of women, who were considered male property. The Jewish creator of the universe, for example—who was and is, bizarrely, a man[3]—commanded his faithful to not covet their neighbour's wives, servants and oxen— which is to say, their possessions.[4]

Young women were the source of egregious forms of civilised social control.[5] Forced or 'arranged' marriages were common, institutionalised rape[6] and child marriage[7] (another form of rape) were common in 'civilised' European, African, Arabic, and Asian societies, where they still occur.[8]

And yet, despite this long and shameful history, of man's oppression of woman, love still found a way, and the individual and his or her community still had some power over marriage arrangements. Freedom still existed, even for women, until the medieval church turned the marriage sacrament into a legal commitment.[9]

This act severed love from its ultimate source in the personal, the familial and the communal, and placed it under administration. Henceforth, centralised power—first the Church, later the state—could wield complete power over marriage; which is to say, over the most intimate relations between men and women.[10]

Love, once woven into the fabric of daily life, became a tool of state control. Desire was pathologised, dissenters excommunicated, families fractured by annulment taxes, peasants trapped in loveless matches, women's bodies policed and the communal joy of partnership reduced to a legal arrangement.

As we've seen, nothing comes into existence without its shadow. In this case the ever more onerous chains placed over a woman's autonomy were counterbalanced with a new medieval GYNOCENTRISM, which idealised woman, and gave her power to command man (where that power did not interfere with the ANDROCENTRIC world).

Gynocentrism was born with the practice of courtly love, celebrated in tales of chivalry. This represented a glorious ideal for man to strive for—the love of a good woman—but it also confined the male psyche, which was expected to serve as vassal to the whims of an idealised, and therefore equally confined, female psyche.[11]

The rise of capitalism and the industrial revolution saw the dissolution of traditionally-gendered bonds, and therefore of marriage. The system now needed man and woman to serve as cogs (physical, working-class cogs, and mental, professional-class cogs) in a new, entirely ungendered mega-machine.

Before this, woman may have been the victim of male social control, but she still wielded real *informal* (collective) power. This was intolerable to *formal* power, which forced woman into a formal world of work, and to live a lonely suburban life at home, estranged from other women, and thus deprived of her social power.

Nineteenth century women still possessed potent forms of informal, communal influence (women's voluntary associations were as effective as they were rewarding), but these were taken from her in the twentieth century when she moved to (in Betty Friedan's words) the 'comfortable concentration camp' of the suburbs.

Woman reacted to her isolation from society, from other women, and from useful work, by demanding to enter more fully into the formal male system, to seek liberation in a far more oppressive prison. Middle class 'freedom', from marriage and modern oppression, was thus born.[12] It was called FEMINISM.

Feminism is the modern realisation of the gynocentric culture of courtly love. The purpose of society for feminists is, as it was for feudal princesses, to enforce and legitimise rules which benefit women; the critical difference being that today's princesses are essentially men, and seek power in his entirely formal domain.

We might say that the shadow of idealised woman's power has entered the light, where it now rules over man with a pitiless tyranny that, hitherto, only men employed in the battle of the sexes. Now that women have become power men they use the tools of man to defeat him, and he is defeated. He is a pathetic, broken creature.

But although the catastrophe of feminism [13] contributed to the erosion of gender, to the dissolution of marriage and to the rise of perversion, all these effects, along with both feminism and 'MASCULISM,' are, ultimately, consequences of the same cause; the rise of modernity and the end of love conceived either cosmically or socially.

What the modern world gained in liberation from the onerous social compulsion of pre-modernity, it lost in intimacy. Treating love as a personal, private state, rather than, as it was, long ago, as participation in a sensuous cosmic order, and, until even recently, as an impersonal social act, forced men and women into themselves.

This fall into self transformed love into a private market exchange of inner states which, over time, has terminated in exhausted boredom and loneliness *a deux*. A society of such relationship is a society of lonely narcissists, or exhausted bores, who pour all their attention into 'finding' themselves in the 'right' sexual relationship.

The immense stress of such a life inevitably forces married couples apart (even as they live together), compels men and women to remain on the treadmill of serial monogamy, and presents nothing but narcissistic surrogates, such as polyamory, homosexuality, virtual whoring and aggressive 'involuntary celibacy', as compensation.

Such a state of affairs meets the needs of the sexless system, which must therefore portray 'heteronormative' marriage as outdated, society as unfulfilling and the idea of a loving cosmos as either irrelevant or ridiculous [14]; because the system needs malleable, manageable, atomised, genderless private selves to reproduce itself.

The technological system, or 'machine', as Lewis Mumford called it, seeks machine people living machine lives, and that means interchangeable, characterless machine parts engaged in functional, friendly, low-stakes interactions. This is the loveless Brave New World of sexfun that Aldous Huxley predicted; the postmodern coupling.

Postmodern Couplings

And so, as marriage and relationship stability stopped being a means of ensuring social order, so elites stopped caring about it. They still recognised the importance of marriage in their own lives, but for the working classes it was neither necessary nor, in many cases, possible for marriage to exist.

Marriage is framed as a personal solution to systemic problems. It would be nice if the working class all tended happy little families at home, but as the demands of the global economy make this impossible—as marriage, like friendship, silence and reality itself, is now a luxury good—the system concedes no place to it.

The right-wing are much exercised by the idea of marriage. When they are not dreaming of commodified sex-objects,[1] they are fantasising about a tidy white world of nineteen-fifties American 'tradwives'—which is to say, the outrageous wealth that American men once possessed to support obedient women in gilded cages.

Women too, those with sufficient capital to have a chance of getting in on the dream—and by 'capital' I mean women with young and beautiful bodies—have similar ambitions, which they sacrifice their youth and beauty, and eventually their lives, in pursuit of. This is the career path of the modern hyper-princess or elite whore.

The physical, spiritual and psychological degradation that such ambitions terminate in for women—the suffocating depression of the caged tradwife and the dead inner life of the hyper-preened elite whore—do not play a part in the capitalist fantasies of women who are, to quote a recent slogan, 'too hot to work'.

Right-wing glorification of marriage, like other 'values' the owner class are happy to sacrifice to the technolotrous god that provides their security, is also a reaction to the dissolution of border, custom and gender celebrated by the postmodern, socialist left; which worships at the same loveless altar.

In other words, there is no hope for socialism either. It is true that in a low-tech environment 'socialism' allows women to choose men for their *joie-de-vivre* or *savoir-faire*, rather than for their economic power, and so it is also true that 'women have better sex under socialism', but at what cost?

Socialism, under the assumptions of the technological system it depends on, does not raise men and women, it flattens them into a human paste. Like capitalism and liberalism, it appears to offer choice, but at the expense of quality, uniqueness and character, which all threaten the smooth running of the socialist institution.

This is why the socialist state (or, the socialist middle-class within a capitalist state) has such hostility to qualities that cannot be socially engineered or redistributed, such as natural reproduction and physical beauty, and why, consequently, advanced socialism promotes bizarre, positively monstrous forms of sexual identity.

The high-tech socialist state doesn't really eliminate patriarchy (or oppressive work[2]), it just disguises male power by turning men and women into the sexual organs of a vast, man-made machine, which, finally, has no need for the gendered human body and must attack any form of gendered physicality as a form of 'fascism'.

And so, neither the ideological ambitions of hyper-paternal caricatures nor those of hyper-fraternal cyphers can offer peace in the battle of the sexes, for neither one determines sexual relations. It is civilisation itself, manifest as the modern technological system which runs our lives, including our most intimate relations.

This is why marriages are falling apart. The modern industrial-technological system ran on stable institutions, and so it prioritised good, solid schools, states and marriages. The postmodern digital-technological system does not; it subordinates these definite forms to the social mush, or SLOP, we see around us.

Much today is made of slop—artificially generated art, literature, democracy and now even partners—but these are manifestations of the social and psychic slop, demanded by technology, which long preceded AI; the slop of our education, the slop of our families, the slop of our hearts, the slop of our minds...

...and the slop of our sexual selves, formed from a society incapable of recognising gender. The reversal of the male instinct to fight for his self, and form it from his culture, and the female instinct to sacrifice her will, so that her self might flow naturally from her mother's blood, leads to the direst social and psychological consequences.

Man and woman either become parodies of themselves or they refuse to meet the challenges of social existence. They choose easy, instantly gratifying homosexual relations, seek refuge in a boutique of digitally administered identities or they give up on love, sex and the passional reality of gender entirely.

Young people in the West are verbally taught to resist the grey-soup of postmodernity, while being rewarded for capitulating to it, for indulging their selves, for cutting themselves off from their embodied experience, for emulating the non-people of the screen,[3] and for living a casual, detached, self-indulgent, half-life in a digital void.

All this meets the needs of the technocratic system, and it satisfies the shallow self with which it is fused. The norm and ideal becomes a sexless, genderless polyamorous 'avatar' with a string of faceless, affectless, artificially-generated hookups at their digital fingertips. This is the spiritual holocaust of high-tech postmodernity.

Eternal Love

'Loving you forever', 'loving you always', 'forever yours', 'forever mine'... How would you react if the person you loved spoke to you like a love song, and said, in earnest, 'I will love you forever'? Many today would accept the declaration as lovely hyperbole, thinking to themselves, 'That's nice, but *technically*...'

Can love be forever? The sober, cynical, scientific answer is no, of course it can't. All love ends, if not in indifference and divorce, then in death. But this is responding to a different question. 'Of course it can't' is not answering, 'Can love *be* forever?' but the more trivial question, 'Can love *continue* forever?'

Of course love can't continue forever. It's usually a miracle if it can continue until the end of the day. The question is, does your love—the actual, real love you share with your lover—exist in eternity? Not, in other words, *will* your love occupy every moment of time forever, but *does* it slip out of time completely? Now?

Does it? To answer this question, it helps to know what time is, and nobody does. Nobody knows what time is because everyone is thinking about it.[1] Most people's minds are constantly focused on the past (in their minds and on the screen) and on the past projected into the future (on everything I want and fear and regret).

The reason that everyone exists, like denizens of hell, trapped in a past-based simulacrum of the EARTH, is because everyone listens to their emotions, which constantly prompt them to go into their minds and look for solutions, relief, pleasure and meaning there, in the WORLD, where reality cannot be found.

Emotion is past, the living pain of the past which uses your brain to perpetuate itself. The emotion you have of boredom, anxiety, depression, anger or guilt uses thought, about all the problems you have and had and might have, to work itself up into more boredom, anxiety, depression, anger or guilt.

Such thoughts and emotions kill the experience of time. You might be a body-bending yogi with 'acceptance', 'presence' and 'mindfulness' hovering on your lips like fruit flies, but if the living past of emotion is in you, you can never know the reality that such exalted words refer to, the actual experience of time.

This is why 'spiritual' people—middle-class priests, mystics, devotees, psychonauts and bodyworkers—are usually such mediocre spirits, with the same strained love lives as everyone else. They hope that a return to the womb (which they call 'enlightenment' or 'grace') will free them of their emotion, but it never does.

If your life is meaningless, emotion will live in you. If you are institutionalised and have (consequently) no real experience of uncertainty, spontaneity and freedom, emotion will live in you. If you are essentially faithless and depend on your position or your possessions for your security, emotion will live in you.

Emotion will live in you if you are dead to the suffering of your fellow man, if you are a coward who cannot say no, if you can't abide in the silence and stillness of nature, if you are incompetent, if you are addicted—to anything—or if your parents still squat in your heart and control your responses to life.

The solution, in all of these cases, is, like everything else in reality, a paradox, two-things at once (wave and particle, light and dark, good and evil, being and nothingness) which, in the moment, resolve themselves into the something or other that actually is, or that must be done. In this case the manifest solution; acceptance or action.

Acceptance and Action

ACCEPTANCE comes first. Only by fully accepting the situation, by turning towards the pain of it, can you respond aptly. If you resist what is, you'll only see and feel your emotional reaction to it, which will cause you to respond reactively, which, as you've probably discovered, always leads to pain and regret.

Acceptance, if profound enough, releases your grip on your self (which is to say your DUALITY—the 'you' that grips *and* the self it is gripping) and allows unselfish consciousness to INTUIT the inner quality of the situation. This selfless reaching, through profound acceptance, into the heart of the situation, we call LOVE.

From profound acceptance arises appropriate ACTION. Empathic experience of the inwardness of the situation does not *react* to emotions about it, but *acts* on whatever it is that the situation demands. I stay or leave, I speak or remain silent, I create or destroy, I work on myself or I work on the other. Aptly.

Acceptance and action are therefore one, root and branch. From conscious acceptance grows apt action. Splitting them into two creates conflict, which the self tries to resolve with reactive action, trying to get or avoid something, or impotent acceptance, monkishly giving up all fear and desire, but doing nothing.

This is the way of the egoic world, which, when it is faced with problems; offers pseudo-solutions, to reactively run into acquisition, consumption, ambition, satisfaction, self-preservation and stimulation; or to passively turn inwards, meditate, pray to God, speak to your therapist and purify your sacral chakra.

In both cases, you are taught to avoid the situation, to either avoid what the situation is and run from it into production, consumption and mindless activity or avoid what it is telling you to do, and blissfully do nothing. This is why both spiritualists and materialists are unable to deal with the situation.

They can deal with the situation under the conditions they reproduce in their daily activity, in the context of their predictable lives, their predictable institutions and their predictable technology, all upheld by their predictable money, but take any of this away, or even threaten to, and they lose their minds.

You'll notice, under the beatific calm and warm smile of the wise philosopher and the mystic healer, *and* under the smug smile of the man of affairs and the professional academic, a certain callousness can be sensed, a certain fear, a certain ignorance; ignorance of the situation, which such people cannot face without their props.

Unconscious people want to have as little as possible to do with the situation. Unless they control the situation, they cannot abide in it; unless they have a script for what to say in the situation, they cannot face it; and unless the situation is saying what they want to hear, they cannot listen to it.

Popular scripts for dealing with the situation include dominating it with one's economic, institutional, physical or rational power (justified as 'pragmatic'), being nice, helpful and compliant (justified as 'loving'), being quiet, withdrawn and unreactive (justified as 'introversion') and being a total dickhead (justified as 'having a larf').

And what is the situation? It is *time*. Not the idea of time, not the half-past four on a Wednesday afternoon of time, not the memory of time—the junk of time you carry around in your head—nor the emotional anticipation of time—fear of or hope for tomorrow. No. The naked experience of time, as it is happening, now.

The Flesh of Eternity

Only now can reveal love, and only love can reveal now. The more I love, the more the two—the love of my consciousness, here, and the now of the situation, there, become one. In this extraordinary—but very simple—experience the simulated idea of time ceases, and the eternal reality of it is revealed.

It is the self that simulates time, the thinking-emoting-sensing-willing me that presents—or represents—reality, in time, to my conscious I. The more conscious I am, the more I can intuit what exists 'beyond', 'above' or 'within'[1] representation, which is to say the timeless quality of whatever I am conscious of.

Conversely, the less conscious I am, the more I exist in the representation of my self, which is to say, in a SELFISH pseudo-reality. I have thoughts, emotions, desires and sensations that are directed towards or caused by the things of the world, but it's all happening in me, for me. I am trapped in a me-shaped prison.

Only by being conscious of my self, of being the I which 'precedes' me, can I reach across to the consciousness, or quality, of the other. Only the conscious I can overcome the lonely time (and frustrating space) that separates us, and that produces all the problems that arise from separation.

This is because *I* am the *one thing*, in the entire universe, I do not have to go via representation—via time and space—to experience. *I*—consciousness—experience that which is beyond time and space—the representation that my self—*me*—projects onto awareness. And that, without separation, is *you*.

I am you. Thou art that.[2] The observer is the observed.[3] The meaning of such enigmatic expressions of non-dualism, common in all meaningful religious traditions,[4] is that, ultimately, there is no time and space to divide us. I and you—indeed I and all consciousness in the entire universe—are one.

Not literally of course. It is impossible to know or to describe this literally, which is why those who are in love turn to non-literal art to express it, why they want to sing, dance, paint or compose epic poetry. It's also why art—great art—seems so much more enjoyable when you are in love, or after you have made love.[5]

(It's also why dualist science and religion, founded on representation, reject both non-dualism and all art which expresses the unconditional love that reveals it. The unconscious purpose of religion and science is not to enable people to experience unitary consciousness, here and now, but to prevent them.)

In the unitary state I experience what my perceptions and conceptions about represented things refer to; their timelessness. Isolated things unbutton their blouses and dance naked before me. Not *sub specie aeternitatis*—under the aspect of eternity-but *per carnem aeternitatis*—in the very flesh of it.

Eternity is physical, and truth is carnal knowledge. The tyrannous king of thought must be unseated and the stony room of the heart he rules from, piloting one limited sense after another, that must be broken open, torn apart, so the sensate universe, in which every thing lives, with a sexual lust to be alive, may pour into my body.

All great artists endeavour to express this truth, as we all do when we reach beyond ourselves into the inner quality of a sunset over Waterloo station, or into a vase of sunflowers, or into a Grecian urn, or into a lover's pale blue eyes and, for a moment, we feel and know and sense that the universe is alive with loving sexuality.

At such moments we yearn to express our love for whatever the timeless quality is that our consciousness has reached into (actual quality that is, not the hollow quality of imagination), but then we start singing, painting or writing, and oh dear oh dear. What a racket! Ability does not match inspiration, and so we give up.

This is why delight at the very finest art always comes with a little twist of shame, that we have not mastered the means, ourselves, to do such spectacular justice to the same inspiration, that such inspiration as we have had, has withered on the vine, that we've wasted so much time merely enjoying the self, or working to preserve it.

Once upon a time, we all lived with direct access to the intense quality of the moment, such as great artists express, which is why, when the time of the thinking mind falls away, and the sense of eternity comes alive, we feel innocent, fresh and childlike. The moment is new, and yet it feels like home. 'It's like a dream,' we say, 'or a film'.

This is how young, innocent children (and there aren't many of those around today) experience reality all the time, before the thoughts and emotions of the self layer over consciousness and come between the naked I and the naked now. As adults, we must work to get back to this innocent state.

And nowhere must we work harder than in marriage. This is not work in the worldly sense of course, a painful and pointless slog for nothing but diminishing material returns, but the delightful and painful work of the conscious man or woman endeavouring to realise their sensual love in the dark world of mere form.

It is easy to be enlightened. Try being married. All the holy-men of the world, those who think they are realised because they have had a dramatic experience, have only just begun. True enlightenment is being in love every day, not with an abstraction, but with reality. And nothing in existence is more real than your husband or your wife.

Vigilance and Courage

Living a loving life, free of misery and anxiety begins then with acceptance and action, with accepting the situation and with dealing with the thoughts and emotions of the self that come between you and it, that fester in your body and emerge as ridiculous arguments, dark thoughts and even deformity and illness.

The thoughts and emotions of the self make it impossible to love the moment, which means they make it impossible to make love with the person that you are sharing the moment with. You won't be able to reach across to him or her. You'll be trapped in your egoic self, in your self-informed thoughts and feelings.

If you try to make love when ego is present you'll find yourself in need of some kind of prop, a toy, or some stimulus, porn perhaps, or sub-dom power play, or a stupid costume. Love won't be enough, the penis will shrink from the depths of the vagina, and orgasm, if it does come, will be hollow and joyless.

To be in love with another therefore means getting thought and emotion out of the way; to be committed to never allowing them to come between you both. This is not an empty promise, something to agree to and forget. You have to actually act to be free of the simulacrum of time that emotion pulls over your senses.

And when must you act? Only all the time. Only every minute of every hour of every day. Just as the price of peace is eternal VIGILANCE, so the price of love is. If you let emotion in, without dealing with it the moment it arises, it will grow, madly, like a cancer. Let enough emotion in, or enough thought, and love will die.

Vigilance is not WATCHFULNESS though, guardedly being on the look out for problems. Vigilance, more simply (more innocently), listens to the quality of the moment, and then, if it is right, immediately acts to deal with hardness, coldness, spikiness, irritation, indifference or whatever else is suppressing that quality.

Lack of vigilance and lack of consequent action let emotion in. If you are not present, if you are distracted, lost in thought, tight with some kind of anxiety, you will miss the emotion as it rises, and, before you know it, you'll be saying or doing something that you'll have to apologise for.

Emotion always leads to apologies, or, if you cannot apologise, to repressed guilt and fear of reprisal. This is because emotion, lost in the past, cannot react to what is happening, which makes it clumsy, inconsiderate, violent, inelegant or deeply selfish, all of which you then have to apologise for.

But of course such apologies are worth nothing. Nobody is interested in your 'sorry', certainly not your partner. What he or she wants is your presence, not your apology. What he or she wants is someone with sufficient spirit to pay soft attention to the situation, and to let go of whatever it is that's in the way of that.

This requires, following vigilance, COURAGE, the courage to act, to let go of your egoic need to be right, to reach across the chasm of emotion, to be kind and tender, and, in the grip of the beast, in the teeth of the tempest, to expose your heart, without condition, to love; which means, to pain.

Love and pain are one. It is painful to love, particularly for man, because the egoic self has to let go of itself, has to die and its *modus vivendi* is to hang on, hang on, hang on. Me, me, me—what about me!? Love takes a sword to the ego, and to its pathological need to be right, to be safe and to be in control.

This is why you sometimes have to fight for love. Yes, *fight*, dammit! You think it's going to be easy? Fat chance! Often it is, perhaps even most of the time, but—again particularly for man—it is also a life-or-death battle with the beast, the egoic pseudo-self that wants to ruin everything. Happiness must be *won*.[1]

And not just in your love life. You must win conscious happiness back from all the distractions that layer over the consciousness of men and women, from work, from drugs, from porn, from obsessive gossip and complaining, from useless consumption, from addiction to the screen and from anger.

Anger is a particular problem for men, but women too have stupid expectations, irresponsibly blame other people for their problems and stubbornly persist in trying to get their way when the whole universe has made it abundantly clear that they never will, all of which are the cause of anger.

Once, with sufficient vigilant acceptance and courageous action, you have overcome your habits and distractions, you will find yourself more confident, more psychologically secure and more powerful, able to resist the emotional demands of others and refuse to be dragged into their dramas and arguments.

Then you will be able to love. This is why life puts people through long training periods before it gives them someone worthy of love. There is no dojo like the world, no ashram that comes close to an unloving relationship, no spiritual teacher who can hold a candle to a miserable situation.

Most people are unwilling and unable to go through the training. They are not just attached to their distracting habits, there is nothing else to them. They are walking talking bags of fear and craving, jostling around problematic selves which are constitutionally unable to look in the one place a solution can be found.

The normal way, with love, is to meet someone, fall in love, have sex and then to endure an ever-worsening nightmare of emotion. The normal way is to take your emotions into a relationship, all your fears and addictions, and then to wilt under the horrendous pressure of having them all reflected back to you.

The normal way is to make love ever less frequently, and with ever less passion and pleasure—perhaps once a week, perhaps once a month, perhaps never—and then to blame the the frustration, bitterness and leaden normality of a sexless union on anything but the actual cause, your disgraceful abandonment of physical love.

The normal way, when emotion becomes so unpleasant that it can no longer be ignored, is for the self to just give up, to SUBMIT to misery—which leads to self-disgust—to JUSTIFY itself—which leads to arguments—and to DEMAND affection and attention—which leads to embarrassing displays of aggression or neediness.

This is all worse than childish. Don't justify your moodiness, irritability or coldness. There is never any justification for emotion. Face it. Don't go into the past trying to decide who was right or wrong—not when there's emotion between you. That doesn't work either. If it did work, it would have worked by now.

There is no right and wrong in love. There is just the egoic, thinking, wanting self, and its absence. If you can feel your emotion, or if you can accept it when it is shown to you, then you can love, because in that feeling and acceptance there is consciousness, which is the end of emotion and the beginning of love.

All this requires tremendous honesty. To be able to sit down with your lover and say, without emotion, 'what am I doing that makes you emotional?' and to listen and to stop doing it; not easy. To drop the old argumentative and defensive self, to give up the emotion and love and be loved, physically; not easy. Not easy, but very simple.

The End and the Beginning

Living this way can only be done together. It's no good if you cannot share the width and depth of life, if one or other of you does not or cannot love enough to reach across the gulf of representation, or if one of you is determined to live more consciously and the other just wants an easy, painless life.

It cannot work like this, again as you have probably noticed. And if it cannot work, then either the relationship has to radically change, into a conscious partnership, or you have to split up. No matter how much love there is between you, if you cannot live together with more and more consciousness, it has to end.

Through accepting pain, through a willingness to be deeply criticised, to one's trembling roots, and through an acknowledgement that one does not or cannot love enough, that this just isn't good enough, radical change is possible, and a kind of rebirth together, which is a wonderful, wonderful thing.

But if not, if you've looked down into the primordial abyss and one of you has decided that you cannot jump, then the one who can will have to dive in, and the one who cannot will have to walk away. You can't stand there together on the brink forever, bickering about which way to go, can you?

No, it's over. That's okay. No love has been lost. Not really. It is only lost in time, not in eternity, which even some of the most messed-up couples have visited, if only in the first moments of delight, when they first came together and rose above themselves and touched something beyond the known.

That doesn't make it easy to split up. Christ no. All the emotional attachment that has built up over the years, all the filaments of expectation and fear that have fused with the other, all this has to be severed, which is an agonising experience, like sawing off your own leg. It's the same when someone dies.

At such times, the ego reveals itself for what it is, a machine built to manufacture suffering. When death and heartbreak strike, ego will *not* stop thinking about what it believes is its absent love, unwilling to accept that the reason it suffers at the end, is because there was not enough love at the beginning.

Just as ego loves to lovelessly suffer at the beginning, by worrying will-she-won't-she-does-he-doesn't-he, and by pumping itself up into slap-happy over-excitement, so, at the end, it will connect everything that happens to what it thinks it has lost, and every thought it settles upon will lead directly to misery.

And how the ego *loves* misery! How it wallows in it, seeking to pull the walls of its self down on its head, so it can noisily wail in the rubble. It groans and it whines, or it turns to drink and drugs, or it goes completely cold, descending into a comforting tomb world of nothingness that nobody can ever reach again.

Some people never recover from real heartbreak (if indeed they ever really experienced it in the first place). They spend the rest of their lives looking backwards, guarded and cynical. 'I'll never make that mistake again!' thinks the miserable entity within that caused the heartbreak in the first place.

Others like to punch themselves in the head over and over and over again. Like a Looney Tunes cartoon, they run from one emotional catastrophe to another, until they expire from exhaustion or settle into the bitter, world-weary self of the seen-it-all cynic. 'Oh yes, love, I tried that once—not for me!'

Some couples exist in a strange state of deepening familiarity and distance punctuated by hideous and ever-worsening crises which, after coming to a head, leave the exhausted pair tenderly okay for a few minutes before ego rushes back in and sets the whole nightmarish emotional merry-go-round off again.

Others turn to homosexuality, or to polyamory, or to whoring, or to extreme promiscuity, or to extreme kink, or to computer-generated partners, all in a desperate endeavour to keep the familiar (literally) at hand while indulging the essentially loveless self in easy pleasures, casual gratifications and emotional titillation.

The alternative is to settle into a half-life of compromise, the parody of love that long-term couples play out in order to indefinitely postpone heartbreak. Comfortable, friendly, efficient, utilitarian; the middling relationship of the spiritually spent middle-minded, middle-aged, middle class; under which a pit of misery seethes.

Who can let their heart break consciously? Who has realised that the 'heart' is not the ground of love, but its emotional representation and so, for love to be, has to break? Who has discovered that the VOODOO DOLL of the represented other has to die? Either at the end of the relationship or in the thick of it?

We cleave to the voodoo doll of the represented other as we do to a teddy bear, through fear of solitude. Thus, to be free of this spectral presence is to live simultaneously closer to the loved other than the mind can comprehend, and, at the same time, infinitely far away from them, and from everyone else on earth.[1]

We have now reached the bedrock of love, the terrifying coldness of the sun, before it strikes the atmosphere of the self. An absolute solitude revealed, finally, in death, whenever the ego releases its grip on the self and allows the light of *physical* consciousness to shine through the represented world.

This is why all great lovers, like all great artists, never stop speaking of love, for the simple reason that, ultimately, there is nothing else to speak of. It's also why there is always something disturbingly solitary in their love, something *not very nice* which doesn't wilt under the pressure of the represented world.[2]

And it is why the happiest couples do not learn more and more about each other, but less and less. *'The mystery grows more startling to the other...'* wrote D.H. Lawrence, *'The tangible unknown: that is the magic, the mystery, and the grandeur of love, that it puts the tangible unknown in our arms, and against our breast: the beloved.'*

This is why those who can really love, are not really afraid of death,[3] because it is only the representation that dies. This is not a question of contingency, but of necessity; for only that which exists in, or is merely aware of, time and space can die. That in my experience which precedes awareness, is eternal.

This is why love is, in the greatest art, so often associated with death, because both are a consequence of letting go of the self. When something dies, its self is taken from you; when you love, your self is taken from it; but the experience is much the same, the conscious experience of eternity.

And, finally, this is why, when someone you love dies, a moment comes, sometimes in the darkest horror of it, when you thoughtlessly, emotionlessly realise that although their represented form is no longer here, the quality of the love that united you has gone nowhere, because there was no 'where' for it to go.

The kiss is eternal.

Endnotes

INTRODUCTION

1   Or the *radix*, the Latin word for 'root' that 'radical' comes from.

SEX AND GENDER

1   Language recognises this, although, being a matter of embodied—which is to say contextual—quality, it is not an exact science, nor could it possibly be. Although *cat*, for example is recognised as feminine in most languages, many varied cultural associations are absorbed into folklore and gendered grammar, so we find, among many other examples, the Hebrew *chatul*, which is masculine gender.

Nevertheless, we intuitively recognise a qualitative difference, which is why we give catty names to cats, which sound feminine, and doggy names to dogs, which sound masculine. Language, the world over, is gendered in this way, reflecting a reality that, before the modern era, recognised gendered qualities not just in people but in animals, plants and objects.

2   The East, for example, as anyone knows who has lived both in the Orient and the Occident, is more feminine than the West, although, as with individuals, culture is made up of a range of gendered qualities.

3   I am speaking of official, left-liberal, postmodern identitarian 'culture'. This is not the place to go into the incoherence of completely rejecting generalisations, suffice it to say, the logical endpoint of the belief that nothing general can be said about men and women (or about anything else) is that nothing meaningful can be said at all. Language

without generalisation is not even a technical concern—as the so-called 'exact' sciences are founded on approximations—much less a tool to express life as it is actually lived.

MAN AND WOMAN

1   Most women know the evil of men, because they've come across it in some form, but all men know it, because they are it, although many are the ways that men suppress consciousness of their devilish nature, or rationalise it away, or project it onto a diabolic other. What this means is that a man who doesn't realise he is a monster is the most dangerous creature on earth, even worse than the man who does realise, but has given into the beast. This is particularly the case if he simply does not have the spirit to do evil, as everyone intuitively understands (Northrop Frye: *'men will die loyally for a wicked or cruel man, but not for an amiable backslapper'*). Conversely, the only man worth knowing is he who has seen his evil heart, been horrified by it, and is some way to facing it down.

2   It also explains why tragedy is a male genre, in that it is about man, born broken, whose split, if he is not conscious enough to heal it, will lead to inauthenticity, self-estrangement, pathetic attachments to an absent mummy and tragedy. *'There is,'* as Camille Paglia wrote, *'no female Mozart, because there is no female Jack the Ripper.'* When woman appears in tragedy it tends to be a 'social tragedy', such as *Anna Karenina*, who does have a dramatic flaw, but who is martyred on the cross of society, rather than on that of the self.

3   This is evident in most worldly pursuits, but is clearest of all in the most prototypically male of these, mathematics, composing music and writing philosophy. Woman's achievements in these spheres are almost laughably trivial. If all the 'greatest' theorems, symphonies and philosophies by women disappeared, nobody—apart from misandrist ideologues—would notice.

The usual argument to the contrary is that women have not 'had the opportunity' to become great. Somehow they have managed to become prime ministers, chancellors, army generals, high-court judges, chief editors, business leaders and heads of every kind of institution, but they can't seem to pick up a guitar and write a timeless love song or a philosophical masterpiece. They just haven't had the opportunity.

This all seems to be most odd, given how important intelligence, music, love and philosophical truth are to woman, until you understand that she is, naturally, not interested in unintelligently pursuing abstract truth very far beyond utility, nor is she abstractly, or conceptually, aware of her own heart as a distinct thing.

Just as it is the critic's duty to bring the soul of the poet to mind, so it is man's duty to bring the quality or essence of woman to awareness, which is why great male artists and musicians are better at expressing her feelings than she is; and why she is deeply attracted to them, even if they are stupendously ugly.

4   This is why depressed men often need to be told to better themselves, to achieve confidence (Jordan Peterson made a career out of this, before he started necking Benzos, shilling for Israel and crying all the time), whereas women don't tend to need this advice at all.

5   The loving completeness of woman might then manifest as some kind of marvellous work in the world, perhaps even something which can be described as worldly ambition, but this is unlikely. Woman doesn't naturally strive as such. She just does what she loves and acquires skill that way. This is why she tends to excel at crafts and arts which demand spontaneous physicality.

6   An extremely individualistic woman would be ugly, and woman knows this—although of course a perfectly

non-individualistic woman (the omniface that really thick women aspire to) is also boring to the point of horror. Likewise, an extremely 'samey' man would be a complete turn-off to a real woman.

This corresponds to 'greater male variability', the fact that there is a much wider variety of male skills and abilities than female. Again, there are plenty of exceptions, but the rule is that one is more likely to find freakish men (including freakishly brilliant and freakishly incompetent men) than women.

(Note that 'individualistic' here does not mean extraordinary, striking or impressive. Women are, on the whole, far more impressive than men).

7   Man makes History, woman is History.

Oswald Spengler

8   A woman need only know one man well in order to understand all men, whereas a man may know all women and not understand one of them.

Helen Rowland

That said, it tends to be working-class and non-Western women who make this assertion. The middle-class woman is ideologically compelled to treat men as friends and equals, while at the same time maintaining that she is oppressed by men, a double-bind which leaves her with no way out but anger.

9   'I am a Woman. I am Furious,' 'Why Women are Mad as Hell', 'Rage Becomes Her,' There are now scores of articles and books on the phenomenon of women's anger. This is explained as being because women are 'tethered down by archaic, patriarchal systems and culture', which is certainly true, but only half the story, the hidden half as ever being that which women themselves (particularly middle-class women; class never comes into these articles) are responsible

for; their identification with, membership of and support for that system and culture, and consequent inability to calmly and compassionately grasp how it crushes men just as thoroughly, and in some ways even more terribly.

We might note here that some feminists, like many of those who depend upon their minority status for their identity, have a habit of avoiding responsibility for their failings and vices by taking personal criticism as an attack *on* identity. Thus, just as a tyrant, sadist or psychopath who happens to be black, Muslim or Jewish can fend off criticism by framing it as racist, Islamaphobic or antisemitic, so a ruthlessly ambitious woman, or one who is obnoxiously loud or viciously 'angry', can take all demands for restraint as intolerable sexism.

10   All women today have a large streak of the police-woman in them. Andromeda was chained naked to a rock, and the dragon of the old form fumed at her. But poor modern Andromeda, she is forced to patrol the streets more or less in police-woman's uniform, with some sort of a banner and some sort of a bludgeon up her sleeve, and who is going to rescue her from this? Andromeda at least had her nakedness, and it was beautiful, and Perseus wanted to fight for her. But our modern police-women have no nakedness, they have their uniforms. And who could want to fight the dragon of the old form, the poisonous old Logos, for the sake of a police-woman's uniform?

D.H. Lawrence

11 The feminist revolution hasn't yet reached the deeply sexist world of bricklaying, roofing, heavy vehicle repair, crane operation, electrical power-line installation, plumbing, pipefitting and welding, which sadly comprise fewer

than five percent women. Oddly, feminists don't seem to mind too much though.

12 This is why in lesbian relationships one of the pair is nearly always harder, more insensitive and more projective—more *male*. That said, as noted, in this world women don't think they need such protection; because the technological system that man made offers it to her, while, at the same time, turning her into a helpless, en-maled and therefore violently assertive slave with Stockholm syndrome.

13 Woman can effortlessly detect the bastard or the coward in his laugh, his gait and the look in his eye, but her emotions, and sometimes her lack of experience, can deceive her, particularly at the start of a relationship when man is putting so much into his performance.

If she pays attention she can see his niceness or his confidence is actually concealing a small and pathetic soul. She can see that he uses technology (cars, loud music, spreadsheets) or power (economic, professional, physical) to augment his little self. Another way to tell whether he is a bastard or a coward is by how he behaves with children, animals, waiters and, especially, his mother.

There are plenty of exceptions, but cowards tend to have bitch mothers, while bastards tend to have doormat mothers The bitch mother corresponds to the kind and lovely—but weak—father, while the doormat mother, sweet and gentle but anxious and easily manipulated, corresponds to the bastard father. These are gross oversimplifications—for status is a complex and contextually-dependent matter (a man can be a high-status bully to his wife but a servile cretin before his boss, or vice versa)—but the basic truism that bitches attract cowards and doormats attract bastards generally holds.

14 PERSONALITY is radically different to CHARACTER. There are still women of character in this world, just as there are men of character, but they are extremely rare. Just as the world punishes the projective genius of man, so it cruelly suppresses the receptive wisdom, presence and innocence of woman.

15   A man who lies to himself can be more easily offended than anyone else.

Fyodor Dostoyevski

16 This is *one* reason (there are others) why women do well at school and university, which involves taking orders for two decades (and therefore starts to seem 'girly' or 'gay'); which isn't to say that women are the only or even the principal reason we live in a world suffocated by mindless formalism. Technology and a massively over-expanded system of iniquity are the chief culprits. The point is that women tend to prefer reform to revolution, particularly when physical security is at stake, and especially when the physical security of her children is at stake.

17 I hope it goes without saying that egoic competition, the kind that capitalism promotes, without either selfless consciousness or the female virtue of cooperation, is insane.

18 It's important to note here that many men, particularly young wealthy men (the kind, for example, whose complaints of being unfairly accused of rape in cases of sexual abuse in prestigious US colleges have become *causes célèbres*) are vile, and treat women horrendously in bed. It is no surprise, now that it is easy for women to get their revenge for this by lying, that they choose to do so.

19 Which unconscious woman accedes to in a tragic and heartbreaking game of 'living up to an ideal' that has played out through the centuries. The ideal might be a manlike mate, or a fuck-hungry succubus, or a crazy pixie, or a demure tradwife, or a pneumatic sex-doll, but whatever it is, woman will deform herself to conform to man's desires which,

being desires, will soon tire and seek something else. Few are the men who want a woman, in all her mysterious simplicity (or simple mystery) and few, alas, are the women who want this, their original nature.

This explains the appeal of porn, which is wholly unmysterious, completely exposed to the male mind. True eroticism, like great art, is founded on implication and absence, not so that the pornographic *imagination* can fill the lack but so that the great heart, which loves mystery, can pour itself into the void; the void represented by the dark, empty vagina, the most mysterious thing in the whole universe.

20 Pornography extends beyond arousing imagery. All spectacular projections of the system, which stimulate the mind while retarding and infantilising the body, are pornographic. Video games are porn, as are most male movies (superhero, fantasy, science fiction), as are all adverts, as is the news, as is moral outrage. Spectator sport, when winning and identification with the team becomes pathologically obsessive, is also a form of pornography.

21 Consider, by way of one example, the fact that Christmas now 'begins' halfway through November, manic exhortations to 'get ready' (i.e. buy something) filling the screens, hyped-up renditions of Jingle Bells blaring through the airwaves, on and on it goes, more and more build up, it's coming, *Christmas is coming!* And then what is it? What actually *is* Christmas Day? It relates to the build up as a sterile, wanked-out orgasm relates to a month of edging.

22 This also partly explains the tragic and theatrical atmosphere which hangs over gay men. They tend to be sensitive creatures, and therefore often very lovely and loving—and of course *fun*-loving—but they are estranged from love.

23 To reiterate, and keeping with the example of male homosexuality, there is nothing wrong with men having sex

with other men, men being attracted to or living with other men, or men holding hands and running across summer meadows together. What is perverse and unnatural (in the same way that eating pebbles is unnatural), is men not being attracted to women at all, men preferring anuses to vaginas (a favourite of many straight men unable to love—which is one reason that we live in the age of 'booty' and 'twerking', fetishised representations of a loveless fixation on the anus) and men being unable to physically love women, and so taking on a compensatory *identity* of 'gayness', with all its predictable downsides; sexual voraciousness, obsessive fear of disorder, self-disgust, pretension, insincerity, a tragic hand-on-brow imitation of sorrow and hyper-sensitivity to criticism. Feminine men who tend to be attracted to men are often the sweetest, most joyous and creative of people—and their persecution was and is the work of emotionally-repressed, pseudo-sexual ghouls—but when GAY sensitivity is degraded into a *gay identity* it becomes a betrayal of love.

Female homosexuality is a *slightly* different matter, tending as it does (and putting aside youthful experimentation) to come less from her inability to love as from her despair that she will ever find a man able to love her.

24 Which gives the cypher (the metrosexual, the homosexual, the transsexual) the feeling of having been *born* the way they are (e.g. 'in the wrong body').

25 'Love' here is, once again, the operative word. Although, as we shall see, marriage has often been little more than a tool of social planning and economic control, the only way to actually free women from marriage within the constraints of civilisation is through technological advancements which, by dissolving the barrier between sex and commerce, more thoroughly imprison (and deform) woman than the most abusive husband ever could. Woman exchanges a monstrous flesh-and-blood husband for a monstrous cyborg.

The dream was that, without having to rely on men—technology can do what man can do, and can free women from the fear of pregnancy that yokes her to him—woman would find herself gloriously free of abuse and we could all enter a wonderland of sexual pleasure. This is not *quite* what happened. Instead, the system 'liquefied' intimacy into a hyper-predatory market system, dissolved the bond between parent and child, atomised the social codes that collective life depends on and pushed men out of collective culture into subcultural sewers; the kinds of places that only rats thrive.

26 Much of this book would strike rural Russian, Chinese, Japanese and Peruvian women—not to mention women of the past and future—as transparently obvious.

27 Women today understand that the 'chivalry' of the past was a pretext for paternalistic oppression—man's endeavour to avoid the horrible mystery of woman, and the demands of being worthy of her, by infantilising her—but in turning her back on real chivalry, she has not freed herself from debasement at male hands, but exposed herself more completely to violence and ruinous exploitation. Now she is just like a man, and so she can be abused just like a man.

28 A woman unsatisfied must have luxuries. A
woman who loves a man would sleep on a board

D.H. Lawrence

29 This of course is an outrageous thing to say nowadays. If you feel yourself bristle, think of ballroom dancing, in which the woman must, in the outer world, follow the man. She will willingly do this if she knows that he is consciously attentive to her inner life (and, of course, to the music of the spheres). Men who are not conscious in this way can be superb dancers, technically brilliant, but women will not enjoy dancing with them. They will feel oddly excluded, or strangely bored.

30 Pity (an elevated form of self-love) and sentiment (cynicism on holiday) are both emotions. They pose as love.

31 Shadow work could not have come into existence before the household was turned into an apartment set up for the economic function of upgrading value-deficient commodities. Shadow work could not become unmistakably women's work before men's work had moved out of the house to factory or office. Henceforth, the household had to be run on what the paycheck bought—one paycheck for the engineer and almost inevitably several to feed the hod carrier's family, whose wife took in piecework, while his daughter was hired out as a domestic. The unpaid upgrading of what wage labor produced now became women's work. Women were then defined in terms of the new use to which they were being put. Both kinds of work, wage labor and its shadow, proliferated with industrialization. The two new functions, that of the breadwinner and that of the dependent, began to divide society at large: He was identified with overalls and the factory, she with an apron and the kitchen. For the wage labor she was able to find as a sideline, she received sympathy and low pay.

Ivan Illich

SPEAKING OF LOVE

1 A flower is one of the most beautiful things in the universe, yet a photo (or extremely realistic painting) of a flower looks tacky, unless it has been doctored, filtered or taken from an unusual perspective. This is why great art is often required to say the simplest things.

2   Power, in this respect—as indeed in many others—is much the same as knowledge. As Balzac noted, 'the mere possession of power, however great, does not provide the knowledge of how to use it.'

3   They either had fractious marriages (Socrates, Heidegger, Russell) or no relationship at all (Schopenhauer, Kierkegaard, Kant, Hume, Nietzsche), or they were gay (Foucault, Wittgenstein), or they were mired in the kind of dependence, sympathy and bourgeois commitment that passes for great love, but which is anything but (Hegel, Marx).

If philosophers had known of the truth that love reveals, they would have written of it, but they didn't, and they don't. Authors of fiction fare a little better—Balzac, Tolstoy, Dostoevsky, Lawrence and several others, despite marriage problems, certainly knew the miraculous reality of love—but it is still extremely rare to see love as it is on the page of a novel.

4   When a superior person hears Tao, He diligently practices it. When a middling person hears Tao, He hears it, he doesn't hear it. When the inferior person hears Tao, he roars.

   If Tao were not laughed at, It would not be Tao.

                                                    Lao Tzu

THE WORLD'S WAR ON LOVE

1   Or SURRENDER (from the Latin *reddere*, 'give back').

2   The term 'material' is misleading, if for no other reason than scientists, who are usually considered to be the avatars of materialism, have no idea what matter is. In reality, matter is a complete mystery.

3   RADICAL GENEROSITY is also impossible in society. Try giving away your company's surplus or devoting your life to service to something bigger than your self (or your self

as reflected in whatever group you are part of). Charity is permitted, encouraged even as it provides a fig leaf for theft, but real giving is a threat.

4   Or God. The immense threat of love also explains why the word 'God' has no real meaning beyond ideological posturing, social work and emotional exhortations to do, think or feel this or that. Real passionate love for anything is an embarrassment to theists and atheists alike.

5   This is why the most furiously repressive members of modern society point to the actual immorality of pre-modern societies (and right-wing 'traditionalists') to justify their denunciatory witch hunts. They are quite right. Just as puritans, past and present, are quite right to denounce licentiousness, perversion and vice.

WHY YOU CANNOT LOVE

1   Naturally, *from* that attention, a JUDGEMENT might then arise—this book is boring, I want to stop reading—and an ACTION—getting up and doing something else.

2   I'm not just referring to romantic partners, but to friends and associates. The self is inherently undiscerning—because all it sees is itself, reflected back from experience—and so it always gets disappointed in other people, which terminates, in middle age, in CYNICISM. Anyone who ever makes a good choice in marriage, friendship or business did so because they listened to something *other* than their selves.

3   If the atmosphere of the house was aggressively sexualised (such as in working-class households), then the child will restlessly hanker for sexual pleasure and attention. This feels 'good.' If there was a cold bourgeois numbness between the parents, there will be a certain insensate distance between the child and its objects of desire. This also feels 'good'. The self gravitates towards whatever situation it learnt to adapt to as a young child, no matter how perverse or painful.

4 Another related reason is, as Dostoevsky realised, it feels good to express freedom from restraint, no matter how violently or perversely. This, something the management class will never understand, explains a great deal of crime and intemperance. Man feels a need to defecate on perfection that robs him of freedom.

5 Boys rarely spend *meaningful* time in the company of their fathers—working together—partly because men do nothing meaningful with their lives, but also because men are generally considered to be at best buffoons, at worst, tyrants. 'Good' boys thus grow up domesticated by women, anxious to please, afraid to be criticised and afraid to stand alone. 'Good', that is, for management, but not much else.

SEX AND GETTING OFF

1 It is even possible to 'hate fuck'.

TWO KINDS OF PERVERSION

1 No matter how outrageously deviant, the sex-world of the professional class is, as you would expect, a managed, 'transactional' exchange regulated by an internal set of laws and 'boundaries'. A good example of this, as Mary Harrington points out, is 'the safe word', a kind of bourgeois contract 'in which authority is only granted provisionally, and may be revoked at any time should the terms be breached.'

THE WORLD IS FUCKED

1 During periods of LICENSE, selves are corrupted by the omnipresent promotion of loveless fucking; everyone is constantly talking about it, joking about it, on the prowl for it. During periods of REPRESSION, selves are corrupted by the suppression of love, which is punished along with sex.

2 Compare the faces of stars of the screen in the 1960s, 70s and 80s, with those of today. This is not just a subjective aesthetic choice by movie producers. It reflects the fact that men and women everywhere have been drained of gendered uniqueness.

3 [Sade] saw that condemnation of 'woman-worship' had to go hand in hand with a defense of woman's sexual rights—their right to dispose of their own bodies, as feminists would put it today. If the exercise of that right in Sade's utopia boils down to the duty to become an instrument of someone else's pleasure, it was not so much because Sade hated women as because he hated humanity. He perceived, more clearly than the feminists, that all freedoms under capitalism come in the end to the same thing, the same universal obligation to enjoy and be enjoyed. In the same breath, and without violating his own logic, Sade demanded for women the right 'fully to satisfy all their desires' and 'all parts of their bodies' and categorically stated that 'all women must submit to our pleasure.' Pure individualism thus issued in the most radical repudiation of individuality.

Christopher Lasch

4 All the regulations of mankind are turned to the end that the intense feeling of life may be lost in continual distractions.

Friedrich Nietzsche

PRIMAL AND CIVILISED LOVE

1 There is a negative correlation between cultural complexity and sexual freedom among foragers. As foraging societies became more complex through intensification of hunting and fishing practices, then through the adoption of agriculture, sexual freedom, particularly of course the freedom of women, typically declined.

2 Paternal power (today we would call this 'right-wing') hates play, the joy of youth, sex and freedom. Fraternal ('left-wing') power hates serious work, the authority of age, self-control and excellence. In a sane society paternalism and fraternalism are subject to maternity; not rule by powerful women (which would be—which is—a warped form of patriarchal control) but love for the mystery she represents, a mystery which both resolves the perennial father-son conflict and intensifies the qualities that rootless (motherless) paternalism and fraternalism betray.

3 The story of love in Greek thought is complex and nuanced, but over time Homer's PHILIA, which could combine ardent love and friendship, became, for the later Greeks, separated into a sexless state of friendship and the troubling emotional turmoil of EROS. Sappho confusingly evoked the sweet depths of the state, but for Sophocles and Euripides, eros was an unconquerable and ruinous force, and for Plato it was a *lack*, a 'child of poverty,' that can only grasp at the shadow of what it yearns for. It can lead to a higher state of ideal beauty, but this experience is bodiless, intellectual, which is why, for Socrates, it was more fully realised in minds of beardless youths than in the body of his wife.

4 Indeed it wasn't considered to be very important at all. It hardly appears in classical literature, and has a minor role in comparison to its position in later medieval thought.

5 The notion we have today of Christianity maintaining a violent separation between body and spirit, is a gross caricature of history which, as Jacques Ellul points out, was 'neither widespread [nor] generally accepted', nor did it form an unbroken tradition.

In addition, medieval thought elevated woman to a position of spiritual sovereignty over men and assumed that the ecstatic loss of self that accompanies sexual love was one of the features of the beatific vision. This, as we shall see, was also problematic, but to some extent it healed the civilised split between love of heaven and of earth.

6 Namely, the Romantic period and, more recently, the period between the late 1960s and the late 1980s.

EMOTION AND FEELING

1 The emotional mind *will* sometimes recognise that it operates selfishly but in much the same way that it recognises that, say, iron has twenty-six protons. The fact, being of no real interest to the heart, soon slips away, which is why when someone is forced to see how their emotions are ruining their lives, they occasionally nod away, 'yes, yes, oh yes, you're so right', and then, astonishingly, seem to have forgotten the whole conversation five seconds later.

2 Which is one reason it is so comfortable with machines (the emotional mind is quite at home in the modern city) and with mechanical styles of thought (enjoying detective novels, crossword puzzles and video games) and feeling (such one might find expressed in hip-hop, or EDM). Note though that MECHANICAL does not mean LOGICAL. The logical mind is neutral; it can serve unselfish reality or it can mechanically serve itself. Thus, the mechanism of the emotional mind, like the mechanism of the emotional world, appears to us as reason's nightmare, a kind of shattered mirror of logic.

3 This is why we love to watch great actors, who demonstrate this oneness to us, surrendering themselves to the truth of the scene. Poor actors, always at a slight distance from the moment, might impress us with their charisma, technique or plummy voices, but they do not enchant us.

4 Obviously I am using the word 'appropriate' in a different way to how it is used in the death cult called 'the world', where it tends to refer to preserving the form of the professional death cult, protecting it from lethal injections of spontaneity, humour, physicality and love.

IDEOLOGY AND HABIT

1   It's also why 'misery loves company', why angry people seek the company of angry people, why drug addicts congregate, why miserable cynics seek each other out, and so on and so forth. Even anaesthetised numbness seeks its own reflection in those it [virtually] associates with.

2   If someone has a bitterly cynical view of life, reality, nature and human nature—not the nightmarish forms of these things, which are indeed terrible, particularly in our grim world, but their essence—they are not to be trusted. They are as untrustworthy as optimists.

3   Or rather, an idea of itself. For the egoic self is indeed to blame, but to see the full reality and horror of this is to take RESPONSIBILITY for it. Self-pity, on the other hand, is an irresponsible distancing from the self, which is seen as a pitiful object which I have no real power over, except to direct sympathetic strokes from others towards it.

4   By 'happy' I do not mean satisfied, gratified or excited. My definition of 'happy' is therefore the same as 'love', an unconditional state which has no opposite. It is not an 'up' to a 'down', not something you can 'get' and therefore 'lose'. It cannot be understood, managed or literally, which is to say scientifically, spoken of. And very often happiness is not even pleasant—happiness, pain and terrible sorrow can, as I use these words, all coexist in one state. See *The Fire Sermon* and John Cowper-Powys' austere *Art of Happiness*.

IMPROVISATION AND FATE

1   Men act and women appear. Men look at women. Women watch themselves being looked at. This determines not only most relations between men and women but also the relation of women to themselves. The surveyor of woman in herself is male: the surveyed is female.

> Thus she turns herself into an object of vision:
> a sight.
>
> John Berger

2   Asking hundreds of questions is a classic technique for avoiding responsibility. If anything goes wrong, it's because someone told you to do it that way. In conversation the abnegation of responsibility is more subtle, you ask questions because you are afraid of taking responsibility for what you say, so you do not really speak at all.

3   Wilhelm Reich argued that deep psychological defences against emotional trauma manifest as surface muscular tension, which he termed 'character armour.' This armour develops as a way to block the expression of emotions and spontaneous impulses, forming rigid patterns in both personality (character structure) and the body (muscular rigidity). These patterns reflect a person's life history of emotional suppression and are expressed in habitual postures, gestures, and breathing restrictions, effectively limiting the free flow of energy and emotional vitality. In the most extreme cases this leads to the mask-like faces and tense, characterless gait of the corpse-like people we call 'stiffs'—although most people are armoured up to some degree, as many women, particularly the lovelier ones, are pre-consciously aware.

Note however that although Reich's extraordinary, and unfairly maligned, work is worth reading, he was a gross materialist and licentious madman, so proceed with caution.

4
> A woman's guess is much more accurate than
> a man's certainty.
>
> Rudyard Kipling

> There is no limit to a woman's intelligence
> provided she is not required to be coherent.
>
> Miguel de Cervantes

5   Or narrow shoulders, long thick hair and the dilated dark eyes of a consumptive poet—whatevs.

6   The various texts of the pick up artist 'movement', with sophisticated titles like *The Game* and *Day Game Nitro*, were either founded on NLP, or 'neurolinguistic programming,' and appealed to men who could only succeed with women by *programming* them; or they were, like so many self-help books, techniques for cultivating a certain appearance, and therefore appealed to women who are attracted not to inner integrity, fine character or grandeur, but to a clever mask.

7   Not so in the past. Old novels are full of men professing undying love to a woman after having known her for ten seconds. Such extravagant declarations are dismissed by modern folk as mad, outmoded sentiment. That there could be some passionate truth to them is simply unacceptable today.

8   This is even true for feminists, who often seek qualities in men that only patriarchal systems can provide.

9   This again is why the screen fails her. Consciousness and the AURA of the moment cannot pass through the gross filter of the internet. Subtle qualities of tone, scent, sensuality and silence die when the internet pulls them from the ocean they swim in. Thus, erotic surprise is impossible on the screen, which can only appeal to calculating thought.

CONVERSATION AND COURTSHIP

1   A *certain* degree of planning can be helpful, provided that the plan is worn lightly and is dispensable.

2   Woman, being essentially unprojective, hates to tell or be told. This is why she prefers not to tell man what to do, why she insists on him showing his worth rather than telling it to her and why projective modern woman, resistant to projective man, hates him doing what he does naturally, projectively explain—'mansplain'.

Endnotes

3   Politically, bastards tend to be aggressive contrarians and conspiracy theorists and cowards tend to be submissive conformists and uni-dimensional institutional men.

4   And into the arms of another; another person or another thing. Men have a habit of running from love into objects.

5   This is a PRINCIPLE, not a LAW. On rare occasions, a loving one-night stand does no harm, particularly to the young, whose reckless errors are more forgiveable than those of the old, and who are more resilient to the pain of casual sex.

6   [Man] must go down into the depths of being, with a string of curious questions on his lips—'Why am I alive? what lesson have I to learn? why do I suffer in this existence?' He is troubled, and sees that no one is troubled in the same way; but rather that the hands of his fellow-men are stretched out towards the fantastic drama of the political theatre, or they themselves are treading the boards under many disguises, youths, men and greybeards, fathers, citizens, priests, merchants and officials—busy with the comedy they are all playing, and never thinking of their own [fate].

Friedrich Nietzsche

THE FIENDESS

1   As a rule, men are only momentarily conscious in the midst of big decisions; they are spirit of sorts for an hour one day a week—which, of course, is a rather crude way to be spirit. But eternity is an essential continuity and demands this of a person, that he be continually conscious as spirit...

Søren Kierkegaard.

SEX WITH YOUR SELF

1   Those who do seriously believe in and regularly act on solipsism we call INSANE, the most extreme manifestation of which is SCHIZOPHRENIA. A softer common-or-garden version of which, the SCHIZOID state, is more or less the condition of modernity. See Self and Unself.

2   *Separate* comes from the Latin for *se* (apart) and *para-re* (prepare); segregate from *se* (apart) and *grex* (flock); but I think *sealiate* would work best here, from *se* (apart) and *alius* (the other).

3   > Is it not obvious that the person who is really in love would never dream of wanting to prove it by three reasons or to defend it, for he is something that is more than all reasons and any defence: he is in love.
>
> Søren Kierkegaard.

4   There is a similarity, in this respect, between making love and giving birth in that both are [now] said to require manipulative techniques. Such specialised knowledge is certainly not to be scorned, nor is the assistance of those who possess it, but you don't need to know or do anything special to give birth. The body will do what is right, if you let it; an idea far more horrific to body-management professionals (a.k.a. doctors and nurses) than to a woman with faith and intelligence.

MALE AND FEMALE SEXUALITY

1   The word science originates in the proto Indo-European word root *skei*, leading to the Greek *skhizein* and Old English *sceadan* which all mean 'split'. The word *shit*, another place that man is more comfortable in than woman, has the same origin. This is why it is true to say that science is shit. Facts are turds shat from the body of life.

2   Again, this doesn't apply to the exhausted middle-aged modern man, nor to the sterile, sexless 'nice' guy of the middle class. Such aphids have very little sexual energy to repress, which allows them to simultaneously nurse their resentment towards and look down their long noses at 'Chad Thundercock' and his bestial buddies.

LIFE, PLAY AND PASSION

1   Life, [according to Ivan Illich]... had become 'a spectral entity'—a ghostly thing. Once an indefinable attribute of living beings and their property only in that very limited sense, it had now acquired the status of real property capable of being owned, administered, and controlled. 'Life,' he [said], is now something 'for which the physician assumes responsibility, which technologies prolong; [which] has standing in court, [and which] can be wrongfully given.' It is 'a process about whose destruction without due procedure or beyond the needs of national defence or industrial growth, so-called pro-life organizations are incensed.' This way of speaking of life, Illich claimed, was an instance of what A. N. Whitehead called 'misplaced concreteness'—a quality abstracted from living beings was being reified and treated as something actual, substantial, and comprehensible.

David Cayley

2   Or a sprightly '*love you!*' at the end of a phone call. Or an 'I love you guys!' tweet to your followers. Or an 'OMG I *love* clotted cream.'

3   Partiality also reduces the whole of one's existence to an objective thing, comprising various objective goals ('fame',

'power', 'security', 'wealth') that are pursued with a fevered neediness which goes by the name of 'passion', but which shatters true wholeness into an infinity of frustrating problems. One fights to achieve fame or struggles to feel secure, but in doing so sacrifices one's health, integrity, trustworthiness and so on. What's more, because such ambitions are substitutes for a passion that one no longer feels, one's capacity to enjoy what is sought is reduced with every step taken towards it. Sensitivity is cast aside along the way, as are creativity and integrity. Even the very things one hopes to get are finally lost. Money, for example, is sought for the independence and freedom from worry it supposedly provides, but the richer one becomes, the more fearful one becomes of losing one's wealth, and the more dependent on others one becomes to secure it.

COURAGE AND SENSITIVITY

1   Sensitivity here means impersonal AWARENESS, it doesn't mean personal REACTIVITY. A man whose self is hyper-reactive, who loses his rag at the slightest provocation or falls apart at the slightest knock might call himself 'sensitive', but he is weak and of no use to woman.

MAN VS. MOON

1   Sometimes you just have to weather the storm. Only a fool complains about bad weather, or tries to change it. Of course emotional storms can sometimes be blown away, they must be... except when they cannot. Then you just have to walk as you must in the rain, for a while, without tension and bitterness.

None of us are perfect, we all fail again and again, we get drawn into stupid arguments and let horrible dark moods poison the room. It's okay, don't beat yourself up about it. Just promise yourselves to do better next time. And for God's sake help each other. You're both in this together.

MAKING LOVE

1 'Distract' is from the Latin *distrahere*; to draw apart.

2 The only *obvious* exception is D.H. Lawrence. Only Lawrence wrote of what actually happens between men and women when they make love, or when they pierce through the barrier of self that separates them. Henry Miller, amidst all his priapic violence, gets close, but only Lawrence, Miller's mentor, could write something like this:

> As they lay close together, complete and beyond the touch of time or change, it was as if they were at the very centre of all the slow wheeling of space and the rapid agitation of life, deep, deep inside them all, at the centre where there is utter radiance, and eternal being, and the silence absorbed in praise: the steady core of all movements, the unawakened sleep of all wakefulness. They found themselves there, and they lay still, in each other's arms; for their moment they were at the heart of eternity, whilst time roared far off, forever far off, towards the rim.

I say 'obvious' because it is only recently that writers have been able to speak of sexual love directly. Anyone who has read Ovid, Shakespeare and Blake knows that they must have tasted the mystery of divine lovemaking.

3 Balzac's words. He should know too. He once saw an orangutan trying to play a violin.

4 Read the Bhagavata Maha Purana, the world's sexiest religious masterpiece, to see what sexual love can really be.

5 Many people feel anxiety about sex, that they will not be able to 'perform'. Actors feel the same. The solution, in both cases, is to not *perform* at all.

6   Jiddu Krishnamurti once expressed a similar truth in regard to knowledge;

> When there is freedom, you can use knowledge and it won't destroy humanity. When there is no freedom, and you use knowledge, you are creating misery for everybody.

SUBMISSION AND DOMINATION

1   Woman has learned to make love through man who does not know how to make love. Hence the dreadful mess that love is in. Since time began she has been manipulated and encouraged to feel that the finest expression of her love is to please man sexually. The truth is the other way around.

The finest expression of love is to have man delight her sexually. This he can only do when he can forget his preoccupation with orgasm and be sufficiently selfless or present in love to collect and receive her divine energies. For him, these are the finest expression of her love.

By teaching her to please him and satisfy him down through the ages, man has taught woman to desire him, to project herself sexually, to make herself attractive to him. He addicted her to an emotional and physical craving for his sexual attention. And he did this by neglecting to love her.

Barry Long

2   One might even use the word 'obey' here, which comes from the Latin for 'listen in the direction of'.

3   The willing, offered submission of man to the woman he reveres, and woman to the man she reveres, the reverence

they both long to receive, but cannot because they are locked in their characterless selves, also find expression in oral sex, an act of sacred devotion. A nothingness to the mind...

> Man, when he looks into the vulva, the physical representation of woman's mystery, sees nothing. But the nothingness is the power of the communication—if he can only look and see without using his imagination or identifying with the old animalistic desire... He is looking into the eye of God in existence. This is where man and woman as separate beings vanish and the mystical union of consciousness occurs...
>
> Woman is less given to fantasy than man and this is evident for her in the practice of fellatio. Given the power, and not the excitement of the penis, the woman knows a great stillness. Her mind and emotions are absent. She becomes completely absorbed in the direct communication. Her self disappears [and] her identification with the act becomes less and less and she enters the place of transcendent consciousness. Transcendent consciousness is registered as a vastness, a void, a blackness or from the point of view of existence, as nothing. But it is real, has a quality of joy and fulfilment, and can't be remembered as anything in particular.
>
> Barry Long

AFTER THE HONEYMOON

1   No? Not your experience? Have you never faced all this? Have you never seen a demonic other emerge in your love? Have you never seen it emerge in your self? Well then, you've

never really been in love. You're either not conscious enough to know yourself, or you've never thrown your whole heart in with another.

2   Not that anyone really has a career these days.

3   See *Self and Unself*.

THE BOND OF FEAR

1   As real as a warm shower after a hard days' physical work, as real as the rush of relief you feel from just catching the train, as real as an egg sandwich.

CARICATURES AND CYPHERS

1   Think of Richard Yates' *Revolutionary Road*, or Rick Moody's *The Ice Storm*, or Ira Levin's *The Stepford Wives*, or Kazuo Ishiguro's *Remains of the Day*. *Eyes Wide Shut*, *American Beauty*, *Blue Velvet*, *The Servant* and *The Celebration* (Festen) and *Dogtooth* are all examples from film.

2   Think of the vapid nothingness of Julian Barnes' *The Sense of an Ending*, or Jonathan Franzen's *The Corrections* or Haruki Murakami's *Norwegian Wood*. The films of Wes Anderson, Woody Allen, Noah Baumbach, François Ozon and Pedro Almodóvar provide examples from film.

3   As D.H. Lawrence noted, the middle class is wide, but shallow. The working class is deep but narrow. One might compare the two by noting the different character of ADDICTION that the working class and middle class are prey to. Working-class addictions are crude, noisy, excessive, life-destroying manias, while middle-class addictions are, by contrast, trivial and pathetic. Professional-class apologist Gabor Maté, for example, compares the heroin addiction of his patients to his own addiction, to buying CDs! This is not to say that one cannot use one's own weaknesses to reach across to those of other which are much worse, rather to note that Maté's wild compulsion goes no further than the record shop.

FITTING AND SUITING

1 Friedrich Nietzsche, surprisingly, understood suiting very well;

> When entering into a marriage one ought to ask oneself: do you believe you are going to enjoy talking with this woman up into your old age? Everything else in marriage is transitory, but most of the time you are together will be devoted to conversation.

2 If you cannot or will not change for the better, and learn to give up your smaller self—give up your personal emotions, your wilful independence, your fears and frustrations, your attachments to familiar comforts and your selfish cravings—you're incapable of living with another, and are better off alone.

3
> I always feel that a man and a woman who do not like the same films, will eventually divorce.

Jean-Luc Godard

A RITUAL OF COMMITMENT

1
> A man can only begin to understand the depths of woman's nature when he surrenders his soul unequivocally. It is only then that he begins to grow and truly to fecundate her. There are then no limits to what he may expect of her... In this sort of union, which is really a marriage of spirit with spirit, a man comes face to face with the meaning of creation. He participates in an experiment which he realizes will always be beyond his feeble comprehension. He senses the drama of the earth-bound and the role which woman plays in it.

Henry Miller

2   Troublesome people have troublesome relationships. Boring people have boring relationships. And people without character either have no relationships at all, or they have a series of trivial—and disgusting—relationships, such as those found in male fantasies of polyamory, nymphomania and Don Juanism.

3   Motivated by biology, as Schopenhauer—himself too jaundiced in matters of love to see beyond this—lamented.

A BRIEF HISTORY OF MARRIAGE

1   Marriage was also a system of reciprocal exchange between groups, not merely a tool for economic (and, inevitably, patriarchal) control.

2   Or no patriarchal control. Women in the fraternal society of Sparta, for example, had more power than in patriarchal Athens. As with all fraternal ('left-wing') societies however, Sparta paid for freedom by sacrificing excellence

3   By the time He found himself in Jewish scripture the Hebrews had ditched the goddess they used to worship—Asherah—who then resurfaced as Shekhinah and Lilith, and then as the Christian goddess Mother Mary.

4   Deuteronomy 22:28-29 mandates that a man who rapes an unmarried woman must pay her father and marry her (treating her as damaged property).

5   Bride kidnapping has also been documented in non-sedentary hunter-gatherer communities like the San people, long before agrarian states emerged.

6   The 'droit du seigneur'—a medieval feudal custom granting a lord the right to sleep with a vassal's bride on her wedding night before her husband—is an infamous example. It is unlikely to have been very common, but it is a conspicuous instance of treating women as commodities, an attitude that existed across Europe, Africa and Asia. Quran

23:5-6 and 70:29-30, for example, permitted sex with 'what the right hand possesses'—which is to say slave girls, who were beyond the Muslim prohibition against forced sex. Untouchable women in India were (and are) also treated as disposable objects, as were African slaves in the Americas. Thomas Jefferson's listed Sally Hemings, the woman who bore him six children, and whom he first slept with when she was fourteen, as 'property'. These, like the many cases of mass rape as a weapon of war, are extreme instances, but across post-conquest societies the law has always fallen on the side of the male in matters of sexual violence. The concept of raping one's wife, for example, did not exist in most of Europe, where marriage implied irrevocable sexual consent, until very recently. Laws that exist to protect woman's right of consent were and are routinely flouted.

7   Child marriage was globally normative until the nineteenth century. The prophet of Islam's marriage to a six year old girl (nine at consummation, according to the Sahih al-Bukhari) is a notorious example, but this was uncontroversial in seventh century Arabia and wouldn't have raised too many eyebrows in medieval Europe or East Asia. In England, for example, Margaret Beaufort gave birth to Henry VII when she was thirteen (the same age that Juliet married Romeo), with similar instances common across the world.

8   250 million women alive today were married before the age of fifteen, mostly in Sub-Saharan Africa and South Asia. Approximately 22 million people are living in forced marriages, mostly in the Asia-Pacific region.

9   The medieval Church derived its centralized authority from its control over the sacraments, but it was the Council of Trent (1545-1563) that marked the turning point, invalidating clandestine unions and requiring clergy oversight. Until then, courtly love traditions and folk practices had persisted, as seen in Chaucer's Canterbury Tales. Peasant 'handfasting

rituals' were also common, legally valid non-canonical marriages, or, in some regions, betrothals in which couples publicly pledged to marry or engage in a 'trial marriage' which lasted for a year before a more formal marriage in church.

10 By the seventeenth century the radical preacher Lawrence Clarkson would be complaining, on behalf of the Ranters, that in 'the repressive ethic that our masters are trying to impose on us, property is more important than life and marriage more important than love'. Property and marriage being complementary tools of one and the same tyranny.

11 [In courtly love] the lover is always abject. Obedience to his lady's lightest wish, however whimsical, and silent acquiescence in her rebukes, however unjust, are the only virtues he dares to claim. Here is a service of love closely modelled on the service which a feudal vassal owes to his lord. The lover is the lady's 'man'. He addresses her as *midons*, which etymologically represents not 'my lady' but 'my lord'. The whole attitude has been rightly described as 'a feudalisation of love'.

C.S. Lewis

12 For all the other women of the world, freedom from marriage just meant more work.

13 Feminism created new opportunities for a tiny minority to rise, while not changing anything in the basic distance between the rich and the poor, so that by the end of a twenty-year period of feminist struggle, the distance between the typically underpaid and the typically highly paid woman was as great as that between low-paid men and high-paid men.

Ivan Illich

14 Consequently, the idea of 'sin' (against the cosmic order), and particularly 'lust,' is just funny to most people. That one injures one's eternal soul by sinning does not make sense in a world in which eternity can play no part, and which rewards and therefore celebrates, gluttony, greed, lust, envy, sloth, wrath and, most especially, pride.

POSTMODERN COUPLINGS

1 Today such pornographic adverts are celebrated by the right as victories against the postmodern left, and even offered as models of traditional femininity.

2 A highly industrialised mass society cannot guarantee woman's autonomy and sexual freedom because its structure depends on the systematic extraction of labour, the bureaucratisation of life, and the suppression of individual defiance. This is just as true under socialism as under capitalist. Socialism may strip the boss of his private capital, but it cannot strip the state of its need to discipline bodies, regulate time, and enforce productive norms. The factory floor under a red flag still demands alienated labour, from men and from women, and the socialist collective must reward compliance and police free (i.e. ANARCHIC) social relations.

3 The screen persona, found everywhere, but most common in postmodern sit-coms (such as Friends), cartoons, game-shows and so on, is incapable of being serious (i.e. is constantly quipping, hyper ironic, etc.), always talks as if it is in front of an audience, treats loveless sex and other forms of perversion as normal and right, is never seen alone, exalts adolescence, upholds social totems and never, ever, does or says anything unusual, surprising or truthful.

ETERNAL LOVE

1 Just as nobody knows what a tree is or what the sun is. They glance at a tree or at the sun and think 'Oh yes, a tree', or 'Oh yes, the sun; I've seen those things before.' As if!

THE FLESH OF ETERNITY

1   Scare quotes because one cannot talk literally of a relation with the absolute. See *Self and Unself*.

2   Or 'tat tvam asi' as the Hindus say.

3   One of J. Krishnamurti's catchphrases. cf. Meister Eckhart; *'The eye with which I see God is the same eye with which God sees me.'*

4   e.g. Sufism, Taoism, mystic 'Nazarene' Christianity, Zen Buddhism, Advaita Vedanta and pantheism. Such essentially NON-DUALIST religious traditions are not founded on separation from the godhead, and so do not depend on BELIEF. They can be contrasted with Islam, Judaism, Confucionism, 'Pauline' Christianity, Pure Land Buddhism, Dvaita Vedanta and atheism, which all posit separation from ultimate meaning, whether this is conceived as a God or as a mechanical process. They therefore depend on belief as well as on various forms of violence in order to 'persuade' others that *their* beliefs are wrong.

5   It's also why the greatest artists describe love as being, in Mozart's words, 'the soul of genius'. Take what Van Gogh had to say on the subject;

> I feel that there is nothing more truly artistic than to love people.

> Love many things, for therein lies the true strength, and whosoever loves much performs much, and can accomplish much, and what is done in love is done well.

> The way to know life is love many things.

Naturally, this advice is lost on people who admire Van Gogh, for much the same reason that people who call themselves Christians never *actually* love their neighbours.

VIGILANCE AND COURAGE

1   What we need, if we are really to endure and enjoy the Cosmos, is a habit of thought that is a habit of war. We must get our malice into our attitude to life and our wicked belligerency into our world-feeling. Our happiness is not something easily drifted into, in a relaxed and passive acceptance of the Universe. It is on the contrary something that has to be struggled after, obtained with effort, won and held by a series of constant battles. These are battles with the First Cause, with Nature, with human beings, and with our own insanities.

John Cowper Powys

THE END AND THE BEGINNING

1   Stopping the apertures, closing the doors,
(In this way) one's whole life is without toil.
Opening the apertures, going about affairs,
(In this way) one's whole life cannot be saved.

Lao Tzu

2   Perhaps only people who are capable of real togetherness have that look of being alone in the universe. The others have a certain stickiness, they stick to the mass.

D.H. Lawrence

3   Sad about departing, certainly, anxious about stepping into the unknown, probably, and dreading the pain, most likely, but the essential, *existential* fear that propels those who live in the represented universe, comprising mortal things, into all the soporific pleasures and phantasmal illusions of worldly existence, no. This fear did not exist for primal people, nor does it for the primal heart.

VIGILANCE AND COURAGE

What we need, if we are really to enjoy and
enjoy the Cosmos, is a habit of thought that
is a habit of war. We must yet our malice into
our attitude to life and our wicked feeling into joy at the world. For the two, happiness is
not something gained: life into it is relaxed
and peaceful enjoyment of the life we are of,
the enemy by something that has to be strung
gladdened, bating it with effort, two and held
by a series of conjoint battle. These are battles with the First Cause, with nature, with
him, oneself and with our own nature, lives.

John Cowper Powys

THE END AND THE BEGINNING

1. Stopping at the aperture, closing the aperture,
   In this way, one's whole life is withdrawn.
   Opening the aperture, going about at his,
   In this way, one's whole life is put to seed.

Lao Tzu

2. Perhaps only people who are capable of real at-
   togetherness have that kind of being alone in
   the universe. The ordinary lovers can't stand it,
   even they flock to the mass.

D. H. Lawrence

3. A labor, learning, certainly speaks about sharing
   just the mill population, probably, and deserving the point, most
   likely, but the essentials of mental that what people share
   why live in the secrets of universe, compassion, and
   things into all the separate pleasures and pleasantness if
   humans of words, certainly, nor this carried upon seat to-
   gramm people, nor does it for the peripheral end.

www.ingramcontent.com/pod-product-compliance
Lightning Source LLC
Chambersburg PA
CBHW011130070526
44583CB00023B/2976